You're The Shift

A whirl of writings to start off your day right

Written by Best Selling Author:

Maria Iskander

You're the Shift

DEDICATIONS

*Thank you to my dear friends who feel like sisters-
Keely, Georgia, and Kiara. You all have supported my
writing and you are the joy in my life.*

ACKNOWLEDGEMENTS

I acknowledge and value the cultural histories, heritage, and traditions of Aboriginal and Torres Strait Islander people. It is my hope that you will join my vision to educate ourselves, our families, and our greater community about unity, understanding, acceptance and meaningful connections.

Finally, I want to thank the Jagera Peoples: the Traditional Custodians of the Land on which I wrote this book.

"You are the Hero of Your Own Story"

Think about it.
You are the main character in your life.
Yet can you remember, being told of your might?

Or can you only recall hearing stories like these:
Stories where women were just as men pleased.
Or stories where women were not even brave.
Or stories where women had to smile and obey.

I for one, remember hearing stories like those.
Nearly all my childhood time.
I remember being taught.
That, these stories, made a woman kind.

Better to be the victim than the hero.
Better to be small in size- perhaps a zero.

But one day, I woke up.
One day, I had enough.
For women- you and I,
Were created for so much more.
Yes, you and I are stronger together,
Braver than ever before.

We no longer, must believe,
That our stories are based on make believe.

We are not damsels in distress.
We are not made to impress.
We do not need a man all the time.

We are wonderful in our own mind.

I hope that the future holds,
A place where women can be bold.

I hope that you too will know,
That you are wonderful,
You are the hero of your own story.
And you are stronger than you know.

"Who are You?"

Who are You?
Who are You really?
Are you just a person
A son or are daughter,
A woman, man, girl or son too?

Are you pretty ugly?
Are you pretty beautiful?
Pretty smart
Pretty hard
Pretty true?

Is your worth from a heart,
On Instagram,
Or a like on Facebook,
Twitter and YouTube?

Single, Taken or Searching.
What is it to them?
What is it to you?
Is a relational status really needed,
For self-respect to come too?

?

WHO
ARE
YOU

"Wake Up!"

Wake up!
Wake up!
For Your dreams
Can come true.

Wake up!
Wake up!
For Your time
Is now overdue.

Wake up!
Wake up!
Let go of pain
Let go of fear.

Wake up!
Wake up!
It's time to grow,
In the rain and shine.

Wake up!
Wake up!
You get one life
Time's up, my dear.

"Six Senses"

Look right with your eyes.
Tell me, what did you see?
A life of some roadblocks,
As much as good possibility.

Listen hard with your ears.
Tell me, what did you hear?
A little laughter, some singing, or silence,
Wishing those we lost, were here.

Smell round with your nose.
Tell me, what did you smell?
From the polluted and chemical world,
To the beautiful flowers and water wells.

Taste the surface with your tongue.
Tell me, what did you taste?
A cake so sweet, a snack so salty.
A bread so soft or fruit so crunchy.

Feel the nature and people around you,
Tell me, what did you feel?
A cool breeze, to a tang of heat.
A loving human, to a lousy cheat.

Awareness of human dreams and thoughts,
Tell me, what does your intuition say?
Aware of others' hidden joy and hurt.
Aware of others' triumphs and cares.

"Come Out of the Dark"

At times I feel down,
Down and all alone,
I want to cry.
But I just can't let go.

Come out of the dark,
You say it aloud,
As I fall down.
Don't want to be found.

Come out of the dark.
You say it again,
I still ignore.
Life is a bore.

Come out of the dark,
I finally accept to see.
As I came out of the dark,
I finally found gold- me.

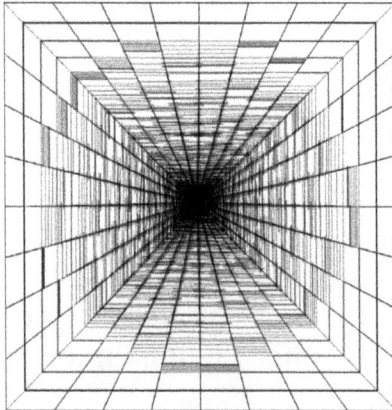

"I Do Not Know"

I do not know if you are a sinner,
Nor do I know if I'm a sinner too.
Yet, all I know,
Is that I lived my life
Lost, low and without thinking through.

I do not know if you are a saint
Nor do I know if I'd ever be a saint too.
Yet, all I know
Is that I have a second chance,
A whole new world
And point of view.

"Be True"

Do not be afraid,
To try something new.
Do not be afraid,
Letting go of what hurts you.

Do not be afraid to walk alone,
For you are better off,
When in line with your values,
And in line with your zone.
Do not be afraid to shine.
In a world of fake dimes,
Be sure to stay true to you.
Be sure to stay one of a kind.

"Fall in Love with a Writer"

Fall in love with a writer,
And you will never die.

Fall in love with a writer,
And you will always shine.

Fall in love with a writer,
And you will find the truth.

Fall in love with a writer,
And you'll find that the writer,
Has always been you.

"Gratitude"

Put on that gratitude.
Let it cover you all over.
Put on that gratitude.
Let it take your heart over.

Put on that gratitude.
Begin feeling joy and peace.
Put on that gratitude.
Begin to break free.

Put on that gratitude.
It'll make your face shine.
Put on that gratitude.
It'll make you age as wine.

"Trust Yourself"

Trust yourself,
Enough to take rest properly.

Trust yourself,
Enough every process completely.

Trust yourself,
Whenever you are feeling sad.

Trust yourself,
Whenever you are feeling glad.

Trust yourself,
To live with a mind that's free.

Trust yourself,
To live your life full and intently.

"Systems"

You were born in a system,
From day one on this world.

You were born in a system
From childhood to adulthood.

You were made to work in a system,
Where you are valued and not shamed.

You were made to work in a system,
That gives far more than it takes.

If your system right now,
Does not always,
Or has never,
Reflected this.
Take this message,
As your divine sign,
To check your system,
And change it.

"Words"

Words have worth.
Whether bitter or sweet.
Words can give instruction.
More than you can think.

Words are funny.
Sometimes they rhyme.
Sometimes they make nonsense.
Words are pretty.
Sometimes they carry a message.
Sometimes they create damage.

Words are more than letters,
Or weird lines that meet the eye.
Words are able to make us,
As much as break us,
At the same time.

Indeed, as you read these words,
Along with other words today,
Be sure to be wise
On what words you choose.

Indeed, may your words gift humanity;
With hope, love, and joy
Gifts that people in this generation,
Desperately crave for, and need.

"One Day"

One day you'll make friends with someone,
One day you'll make enemies with a lot.

One day you'll say you're doing just fine.
One day you'll say you're actually not.

One day you'll feel like you've had enough.
One day you'll feel like you've gotten tough.

One day you'll be feeling undeniably miserable.
One day you'll be feeling undeniably incredible.

One day you'll see life making you real mad.
One day, you'll see life making you real glad.

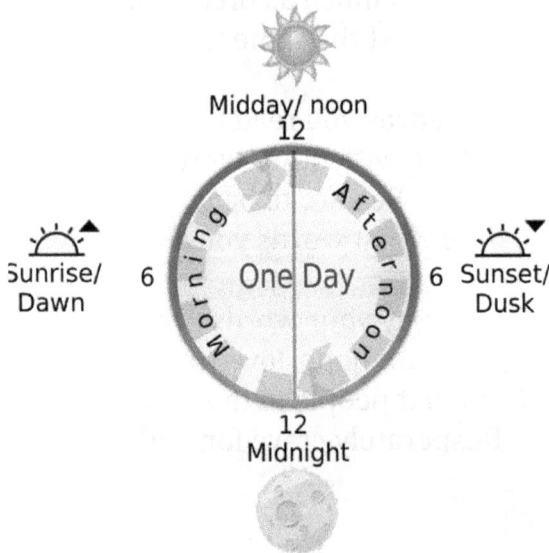

Midday/ noon
12

Sunrise/ Dawn   6   Morning   One Day   Afternoon   6   Sunset/ Dusk

12
Midnight

"Your Mother, as Mine"

There is no greater good, in our way,
Than the motherhood we cherish today.
From mothers past, present and soon to be;
A mother's love is a taken blessing, for you and me.

Now, your mother as mine, is the epitome of sacrifice.
Indeed, your mother as mine, is truly one of a kind.
Yes, your mother as mine, is strong amid sadness,
True, your mother as mine, is a source of gladness.

Thus, in the world we have now seen,
Where people can be sly and sorta mean,
Your mother's love, as mine, is a source of insight;
Albeit a gate, to open our blinded eyes.

With eyes wide open from our mothers' love,
You and I, can become renewed inside out.

From body, spirit, and soul,
Your mother, as mine, can inspire us from the heart.
With such inspiration, you and I can;
Accomplish anything, leave a legacy,
And become a better woman or man.

Thank you,
Mom

"You were never the One"

Been looking forward to grow up,
So that I could be in your gang.
Always noticed you all there, so close
Made me wishin' to have that closeness then.
But as I grew up,
I came to realise that,
You were never the one,
That I wished I had.

Used to admire your jokes,
Thought you were like no one.
Someone kind, brave,
With love enough for everyone.
But as I grew up,
I came to realise that,
You were never the one,
That I wished I had.

Remembered how I put myself down,
So you could feel welcomed in.
Thought to show you around ,
Treated you as one of my kin.
Felt honoured to have you in my life,
So, I'd welcome you, at any time.
But as I grew up,
I came to realise that,
You were never the one,
That I wished I had.

Indeed, as I got older,
I came to realise that,
You're good from far away;
Your life was just for play.
And you were never the one,
That I wished I had.

"Euphoria"

Euphoria.
Greek Word.
Used for describing our wellbeing,

Euphoria.
Rare Word.
For feeling an excitement unseen.

Euphoria.
Complex Word.
Used for the liberation of our pain.

Euphoria.
Shiny Word.
For feeling happy in the mundane.

"Can we Just Talk?"

Teach me something.
Tell me about your life.
Challenge my way of sight.

Tell me something.
Your experiences and lessons.
Make me want to listen.

Move me to discuss the deep;
From the hard stuff,
To things that make us creep.

Discuss with me psychology;
Of this life and the humans we see.
Inspire me to join you,
In your depth and authenticity.

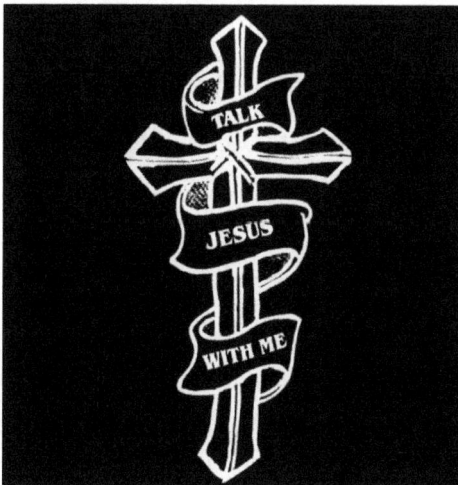

"Good Day to You, Boo"

May blessings, joy, and peace,
Come your way superstitiously.

Today and every time.
May it be a good day to you, my boo,
For there is no one like you.

Indeed, you are more precious than gold.
And don't you forget that,
From this young age,
To when you grow old.

Yes, whatever it is.
No matter the biz,
Or whatever the shiz,
I hope you will find hope,
Thereby remembering how you're dope.

Really, you're worthy,
And deserving,
Of only the very best,
And even when you're hurting.
I hope you're working,
On feeling yourself again.

So, may this be a gentle reminder,
That no matter what you do;
There's someone praying,
And wishing a good day to you, my boo.

"That This World Will Show You That"

Wonder what it will be like,
To get away with whatever?
A 'green card' if you will, to be selfish,
Not show a care or know better?
Well, you can be assured as a fact,
That this world will show you that.

Have you ever tried to live the dream?
Whatever that may be for the country?
Then, in a blink of an eye,
You find yourself living that dream,
But still feel empty inside.
Certainly, you can be assured as a fact,
That this world will show you that.

Considered what you would feel like,
If you had the chance to live your life?
A life where money is no problem,
Surplus and burnout is considered normal.
To add, to get your way in everything,
Even if it means you'll have to sin.
For sure, you can be assured as fact,
That this world will show you that.

"Lies"

Lies going round and round.
Lies making noise around.
Lies sounding sweeter than truth.
Lies binding people to lose.

Lies are said to and fro.
Lies are said for a show.
Lies are used- black and white.
Lies are present at hindsight.

But no one tells you what lies do.
As lies trap one and keep one down.
Whereas the truth gives one life,
Purpose and freedom, all round.

"Being the Bee"

You don't need to worry,
You don't need to fret.
You don't need to get upset.

For you're a trauma survivor.
So, chances are, you're hard on yourself too.
Although you mean a lot to people.
You carry the internal pain with you.

Others too often live on the outside.
Indeed, others too often live for themselves-
seldom change.
Yet, we should be like bees searching for the
goodness.
In contrast with the 'flies' of people, that stick to the
rubbish.

Therefore, I pray that you dear reader, will
start to see,
The way others see you, from now and always.
And may you manifest the life of "Being the Bee";
For in that, you'll see the good in life and everybody.

" You"

You are precious.
You are pure.
You are cherished.
You are true.

No need to worry for tomorrow.
For tomorrow will provide.
No need to worry in pleasing people.
For no one can be pleased, all the time.

I hope you remember how since your birth,
You're made for a purpose:
You've got an irreplaceable kind of worth.

" What are You Hungry For?"

What are you hungry for?
A life filled with truth,
Or a life following the rest?

What are you hungry for?
People who benefit your exterior look,
Or people, who inspire you to reach your best?

What are you hungry for?
A life with no challenges to grow,
Or a life that motivates you to soar?

What are you hungry for?
Narratives in your mind that criticise and complain,
Or narratives that are hopeful and inspiring change?

"Trust Yourself"

To trust yourself is a hefty measure.
Especially when we're taught no better.
Indeed, the society we live in profits much,
In our insecurities, doubts, and such.

Yet, more and more research does show,
That self-compassion and trust in oneself,
Is the way to go.

From eating healthily and changing bad habits,
Trust yourself to incorporate a healthy practise.
For beating yourself for the failures, is never helpful.

So, dear reader, I plea with these words;
For you to swap out the self-recrimination.
In place with self-love and compassion,
And thereby be able trust yourself- on every
occasion.

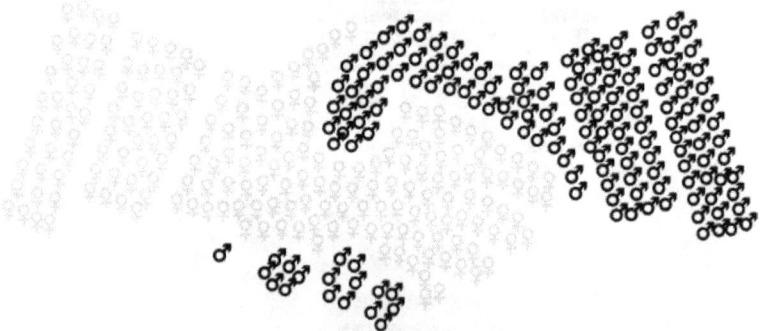

"Inner Beings"

We all have an 'inner owl'.
An urge that tries us to make us doubt.

We all have an inner feral cat.
A voice that tries to make us lash.

As Metamorphosis strikes again.
You and I can change from within.

We all have an inner loyal pet.
A strike to work for the best.

We all have an inner spirit inside.
A calling to walk humbly, at all times.

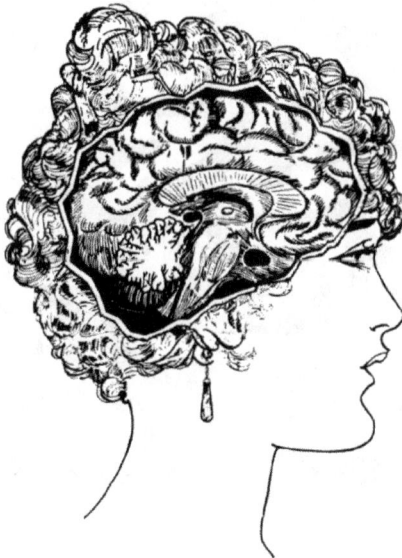

"Fulfilling our Intents"

We get our babies back to the nest.
We launch them safely as we know best.
We even learn to take better care of ourselves.
We move closer and closer, to coming out of
our shells.

Indeed, as this happens- a universal 'shell
breakthrough';
We take the road to fulfilling our intents- without
further ado.

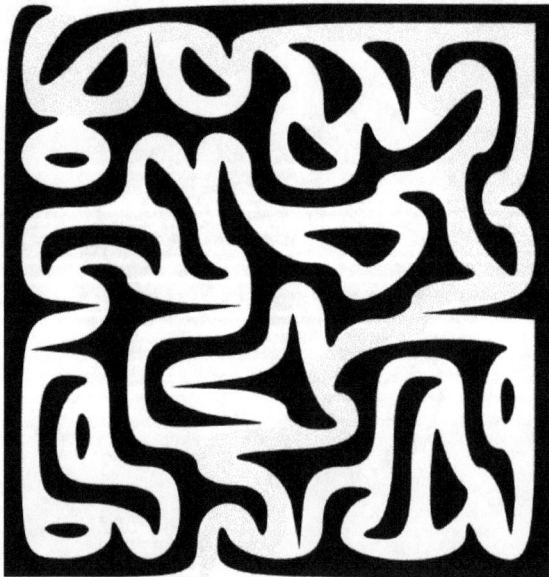

" Take Care"

Take care of your thoughts today.
Take care of the words you say.
Take care when no one else may do.
Take care to be the best version of you.

"Create"

Create a life that feels like what you envision.
Create a life filled with love, purpose and meaning.
Create a life with only your permission.
Create a life where you leave a legacy for years end.

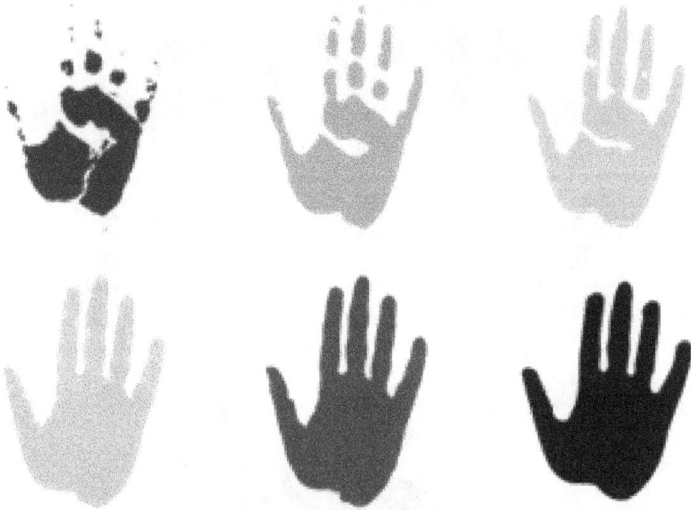

"Help"

You and I will survive and thrive by help:
Selfless help from people around us,
Both family and friends.
Miraculous help from willing strangers,
Who we may never see again.

Clearly, you and I are made for so much more.
Thus, don't be prideful to not accept love,
Or generous help of those that show up.

For by accepting what is and what help arrives,
You and I will inevitably survive and thrive.

"Magic Manifestation"

Every once in a while, you'll find that a gift will
come through.
A gift magically manifested from the universe
A gift made intentionally for only you.

And much like the magic words you see and
read about;
From Expecto Patronum, Acradabra, and thank you-
no doubt;
Your new magic manifestation will come to
you today:
So be sure to accept it- remaining brave.

"Just Do it- Now"

We've all heard in a number of ways,
How inspiration can be found or made.
Yet, do you ever consider what to do,
When life throws its daggers at you?

As tide rises each day,
In accordance to the moon.
Have you ever thought of the opportunities,
Where you may daily pass through?

Indeed, more often than not,
We reach a plateau of some kind,
In our body, soul and spiritual inclines.
In other words, miracles happen everyday.
You and I are a living, breathing one.

So, it is up to you and I to seize the day,
Thereby seeing all the miracles;
That God and His universe, are sending your way.

"Let it Be"

Let it be.
Let it be.
Let it be.
Let it be
Words that come to hurt you.
Let it be.

Let it be.
Let it be.
Let it be.
Let it be.
People that turn against you.
Let it be.

Let it be.
Let it be.
Let it be.
Let it be.
The hard times and wonderful blessings.
Let it be.

"Heal Through"

This world will push you down.
This world will cause you pain.
This world will take you around.
This world will make you ashamed.
This world will promise lies.
This world will test your faith.
This world will take sides.

All in all, the world will drive one insane;
As much as make one feel restless the same.
Yet, despite what this world puts you through,
You and I, can decide:
Whether to wallow in despair,
Or heal through everywhere.

BE·STEADY

"Forgive Them"

People will spread rumours.
People will spread lies.
People will wish you were stupid.
People will wish you'd take their sides.

During the stressors from such people,
Be sure to not carry it,
But rather to forgive them.
As these kinds of people, are mean
From their low self-esteem;
And like a broken-down car,
These people need a mend.

" I Didn't Expect to Care This Much"

I didn't expect to care this much,
For the people and things of this world.
I didn't expect to care this much,
To feel loved, appreciated and heard.

I didn't expect to care this much
For building a life where I'm financially free.
I didn't expect to care this much,
To be a part of something bigger than me.

" I am a Woman"

I am a woman.
Who is nothing more and nothing less.
I am a woman.
Who tries her very best.

I am a woman,
Who has laughed and who has cried.
I am a woman,
Who will help others to reach the skies.

I am a woman,
Who beats to the rhythm of a drum.
I am a woman,
Who loves to be kind to everyone.

"My Bad"

I saw the world in cherry ripe.
A technicolour of people who'd do right.
Yet, I soon learned that it was my bad- I confess;
To assume a world far better in my head.

"Sweetheart"

You are something to admire.
An original with no sample.

You are something like no other.
A heart of love and gold.

Yesterday may be history,
Tomorrow may be a mystery.
But for what I know now to be:
You have a heart of gold,
A sweetheart like none have seen.

"You are Here"

You are here to walk humbly.
You are here to show mercy.
You are here to keep the good fight.
You are here to do what is right.

"You will have Me"

If the world forgets you sometimes,
Just know that you will have me.
Yes, you will always have me;
From now on,
'Til the end of our lives.

"You Were Born to be Wild"

Some people will never appreciate you.
No matter what you may do.
Yet, please, do not cry or fret.
For such people will not accept.

Some people will prefer the rain.
No matter what you may say.
So, do not be disheartened child.
For you were born to be wild.

"Open Mercy"

May you receive open mercy.
May you find a hidden grace.

May you receive open mercy.
May you experience a pure taste.

May you receive open mercy.
May a smile take over your face.

May you receive open mercy.
May you find help in every place.

"I Think......... I Think Too Much"

The act of thinking is important for you and I.
The act of thinking helps make sense of our lives.
The act of thinking can inspire us to set our groove.
The act of thinking- sometimes too much, can carry
us through.

"Break free"

Break free from your doubts that weigh over you.
Break free from the people that drain you.
Break free from the stories that make you upset.
Break free from the narrative that is in your head.

As you break free from what holds you back.
You will find a breakthrough that shows:
The better version of you-someone, you have not
yet, met.

"Be Composed"

Be composed in all virtues.
Be composed in every right.
Be composed with a firm purpose.
Be composed of soul and body alike.

Be composed with prayer so often.
Be composed to suffer and not smite.
Be composed to be angry.
Be composed to not cause strife.

Be composed to live meekly.
Be composed to stay lowly of mind.
Be composed to good will living.
Be composed to always be kind.

" Qu'e Sera' Sera'"

Whatever will be, will be.
The future is not ours to see.
So why worry about what will happen?
For whatever will be, will be.

"That is Us"

We love.
We fight.
We test.
We cry.
We argue.
We sin.
We lose.
We win.

But despite all that,
There remains this fact:
That all the ups and downs,
Changes from then and now,
That is us.
With no shadow of doubt.

"Protect Your Peace"

Do as you please.
But ensure to think through,
For all works, you intend to do.
So that in doing so, you'll find ease.
Thereby, protecting your peace.

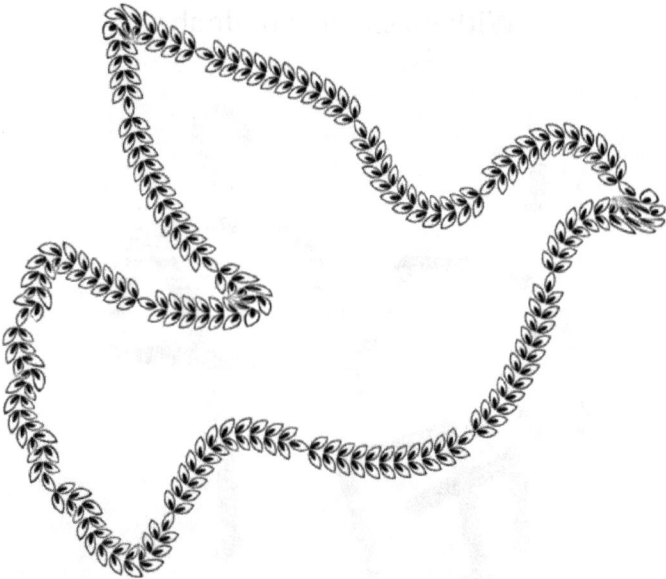

" Be Drawn to do What is Right"

Surely all works are not the same.
Some works please God.
Whilst some are insane.

So, whatever you find in life.
May your heart grow enough.
To be drawn to do what is right.

"You are Enough"

You are enough.
Take off the shame.
You are enough.
No need to complain.

You are enough.
Even when others don't see.
You are enough.
Begotten, just, and worthy.

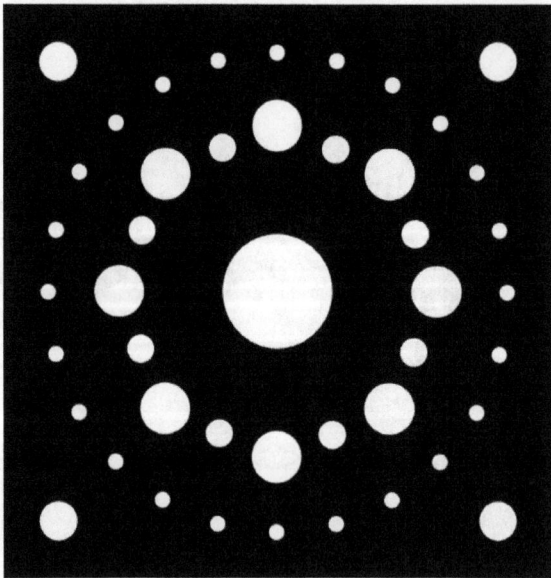

"Who Else?"

Tell me who else,
Can hug me like you do?

Tell me who else,
Can love me like you do?

Tell me who else,
Can see me from now.

Tell me who else,
Can take away my doubt.

"Be Free"

Be free from your own self-will.
Be free.

Be free from the work that chills you.
Be free.

Be free from those who hate you.
Be free.

Be free from what the world views.
Be free.

Day 53/365

"Feed Yourself"

You cannot continue to depend on others to feed you.
You must learn to feed yourself.

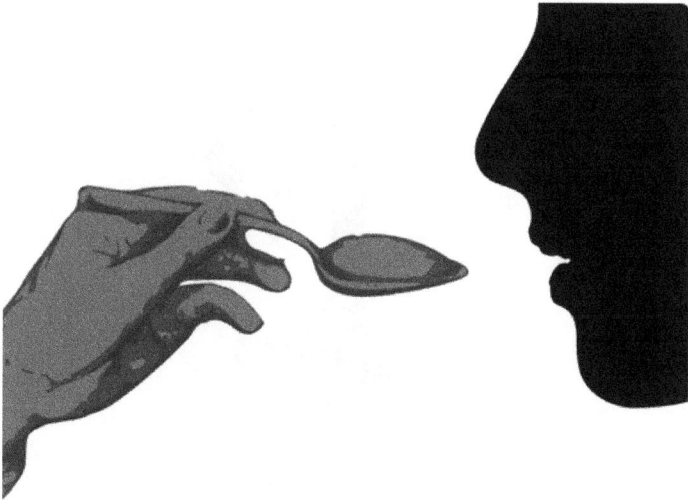

"Choose"

Today, you have the chance to decide;
Whether to live broken,
Or blessed from this time.

So, it is my hope that you'll choose;
To live blessed,
With nothing to lose.

CHOICES

" Unshaken"

Even though there were,
Are.
Or will be.
Thousands of people,
Against you.
Whether literally.
Or figuratively.
Know.
Just know.
You are amazing,
Keep.
Just keep.
Your faith unshaken.

"Keep"

Answer those who will to call.
Keep them when in distress.

Catch those before a fall.
Keep them with your goodness.

Commune with your own heart,
Keep them safe like the rest.

Stand in awe and sin no more.
Keep them with your gladness.

Have mercy on the small.
Keep them in your countenance.

"In peace, sleep"

In peace, will I both lay my head down and sleep.
For You alone, make me dwell with ease.

"Remember Me"

Remember me O Lord when You come into
your Kingdom.
Remember me O King when You come into
your Kingdom.
Remember me O Holy when You come into Your
Kingdom.
Remember me O Almighty when You come into
Your Kingdom.

"To You is the Power"

To You is the Power.
The Glory.
The Blessing.
And the Honour.
Forever.

To You is the Power.
The Mighty.
The Blessing.
And the Honour.
Forever.

To You is the Power.
The Redemption.
The Blessing.
And the Honour.
Forever.

"If I ruled the World"

If I ruled the world,
I'd throw all the money,
Out in the air,
Like you'd do with confetti.

If I ruled the world,
Everyone would have a home,
Have great nutritious food,
To live life with no worry.

If I ruled the world,
A fashion of kindness all round,
Would come with no bound,
Paving paths to the Glory.

" Morons"

Scientists got it right,
When they said our world was made
Electrons, neutrons and protons- the same.

Yet, the scientists fell short to see,
Or to mention how,
Our world is also made,
With a bunch of morons
That drive us all insane!

" Don't"

Don't let your heart be troubled.
Don't let your heart be afraid.
Don't let your heart stay broken.
Don't let your faith wither away.

" Whispers"

The man who whispers against his neighbour,
Is like a serpent from the story of Adam and Eve.

The man who whispers against his neighbour.
Condemns the soul of the listener, equally.

The man who whispers against his neighbour,
Drags himself to gnash their teeth, eternally.

"Reach"

Reach for the Heaven and the skies.
Reach for the faithful, all the time.

Reach for the righteousness inside out.
Reach for the justice in your mouth.

Reach for the man, weak and strong.
Reach for the man who wants to belong.

"Happy are Those"

Happy are those who are poor,
For they'll realise that God isn't far.

Happy are those who grieve,
For they'll be comforted with peace.

Happy are those who hunger through,
For they'll be willed with virtue.

Happy are those who are merciful,
For they'll always look so beautiful.

Happy are those whose heart is pure,
For they'll be strong to endure.

Happy are those who work for peace,
For they'll find who they're meant to be.

Happy are those who are persecuted today,
For they'll live with no ounce of shame.

"See You, my Friend"

See You, my Friend,
Now.
It is time to go.

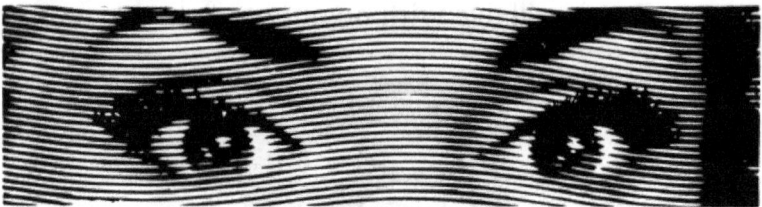

"Be-attitude"

The positive attitude doesn't come easily.
At times, it's more natural go quickly.
But as you can change,
You will be sure to see;
That there's be-attitude people,
In you and in me.

"Clothe Yourself"

Clothe yourself with compassion.
Wrap yourself with kindness.

Clothe yourself with humility.
Carry yourself with gentleness.

Clothe yourself with patience.
Speak to yourself with love.

Clothe yourself with humanity.
Take care of yourself from the heart.

"Even When"

Act with sole integrity,
Even when you feel burnt out.

Have a lot of compassion for people.
Even when the darkness may doubt.

Give out your warmest empathies.
Even when you want to scream and shout.

Be kind with yourself and be brave,
Even when others detest your name.

"Confucius Quotable"

A great man is hard on himself; a small man is hard on others.

"Do not be Afraid"

Do not be afraid Daniel.
For as the lion comes and prowls.
The hand of the Lord,
Is with you all around.

Do not be afraid Giovanni.
You are named after John to see.
The divinity of the Lord,
In you and in everybody.

Do not be afraid Dimitri.
For as the former pope, you'll see:
How the mercies of the Lord,
Will make you strong quickly.

Do not be afraid Arsanius.
You are named after a modern martyr;
Living proof that the Lord is hereafter,
With you now, and forever after.

"Pope Shenouda III Quotable"

If you have nothing to give people, give them a warm smile and a kind word. Give them love, give them tenderness, give them a word of encouragement; give them your heart.

"Imagine"

Ever feel discouraged about the future of the world
we live in?
I've been there too,
I can promise you that.
Yet, why don't we imagine that now,
At this very time,
There is a girl and boy reading a book:
A book about brave kids,
Battling evils of all kinds.
And from that moment of reading,
A pure bliss,
The betterment of our world's future;
Are being planned- by these very kids.

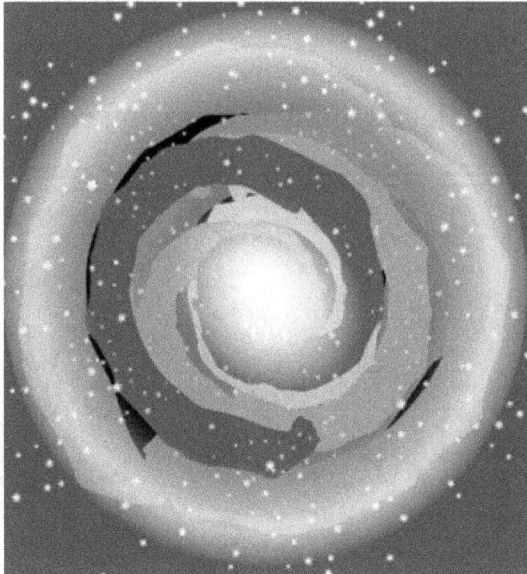

"Amma Quotable"

Be like the honeybee who gathers only nectar wherever she goes. Seek the goodness that is found in everyone.

"St Nektarious Quotable"

Do not let anything deprive you of hope.

"When you Feel"

When you feel sad, go for a walk outside.
Spend some time with your family and friends.
Be sure to have a good time.

When you feel angry, do some cardio.
A little bit of dance, a little bike or run.
Move your body the way you like to go.

When you feel tired, turn off all screens.
Be sure to give a little detox from the digital.
Then invest in real funny and loving human beings.

When you feel anxious, just observe your thoughts.
Take examination and write it all down;
Perhaps in a private journal of sorts.

When you feel uninspired, try something new.
Go for a walk or give a gift away.
Try to spread the good from you.

When you feel self-doubt, celebrate a win.
Then identify your limiting beliefs inside,
To learn how to make for yourself, a new life.

When you feel irritated, get moving on.
Carry your breathing intentionally,
Turn up the music to your favourite song.

"You Are Not Alone"

God's spirit empowers.
God's spirit gives you strength.
God's spirit walks with you.
God's spirit is your constant friend.

"When in Distress"

Tremble and do not sin.
From your going in,
To your going out.
Search your heart,
Be responsible
Keep silent.
Then, in peace lie down,
And sleep,
Knowing that the Lord'll,
Make you dwell in safety.

" Real"

In our present day and age
We may have seasons of doubt.
Seasons of not being honest with God,
And mucking all about.

Instead of taking our burdens to Him,
We try to make it through ourselves.
Which as a result, will leave us with:
The harm and pain, throughout.

So, we have a choice to make like David
Will we wallow in our depression,
Anxiety, fears, and troubles alike?
Or will we carry FAITH to the God,
Who sees us all the time?

"Today"

Today, I choose to be like Daniel,
Jesus, and the Apostle Paul.

Today I aim to find God,
In prayer and in every place I go.

Today I ask for mercy on me,
From the gracious God alone.

Today, I know I am weak;
So, I ask for healing to the bone.

"Heal Me"

O Lord, heal me, for my bones are troubled.
O Lord, heal me, for my soul is troubled

O Lord, how long?

"Weary"

I declare my weariness,
I declare my tiredness in prayer.
I am weary with my groanings,
I drench my couch with my tears.

I declare my weariness,
I declare my most transparent places.
I am weary with my pain and tribulations,
I shove my feelings down, can't deal anymore.

I declare my weariness,
I declare hope from this one truth.
I am weary with my burdens thrown on me.
I am weary in what others around me do.

"Live Your Life"

Live your life closely. Provide vision, direction, and correction.

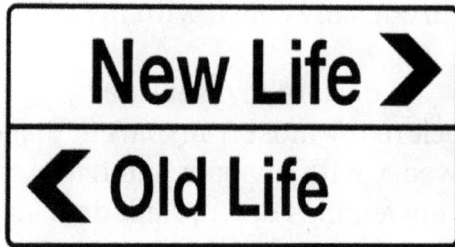

```
┌─────────────────────┐
│  New Life  ❯         │
├─────────────────────┤
│  ❮ Old Life          │
└─────────────────────┘
```

Day 84/365

"Chapters"

You can't skip chapters.
You can't pause.
Or even rewind.

You can only read each chapter,
Go through it,
Line by line.

You won't enjoy every chapter.
Some characters you'll love.
Others you'll wish weren't around.

Some chapters will feel like Hell.

While some will make your heart well.

Yes, you won't enjoy every chapter.
There'll be moments you'd rather skip,
Not read.
But at the same time,
There'll be moments that you'll love,
As much as cherish to keep.

At the end of the day,
You got to keep going.
As your chapters make a story:
A story that's one in a million.
And that makes the world, less boring.

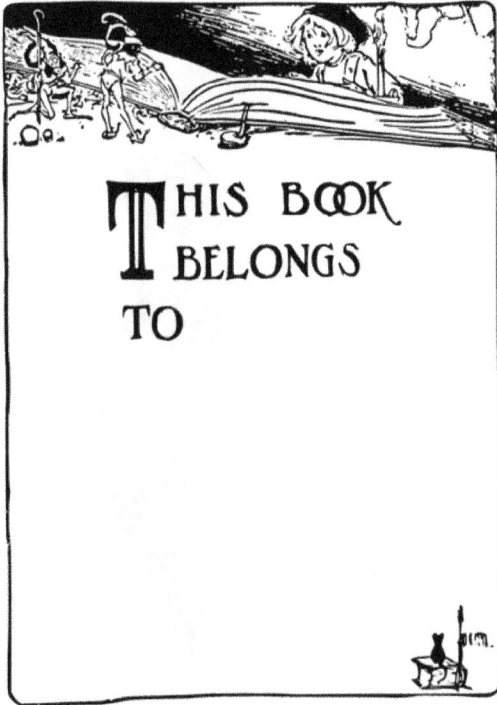

THIS BOOK
BELONGS
TO

"Guard Me"

I acknowledge my need for You today.
I pray that You would breathe peace my way.
Fill me through Your Holy Spirit.
Would You guard my heart too?
Show me how much I am strong,
When I am right beside You.

"Trust in You"

I put my trust in You today.
Anxious thoughts are taking over.
My mind is spread and spent all over.
It's easy to take my eyes off of You.
So, when I feel afraid,
Remind me to put my trust in You.

"Protect"

Protect your mind,
And others too.
Protect your heart,
And make others move.

Protect your body,
And fall back on your strength
Protect your name,
And be equipped to start again.

"Thank You"

Thank You for this truth.
Thank You for the gifts too.
Thank You for easing my mind.
Thank You for taking my time.
Thank You for reminding me always.
Thank You for counting up my days.

"Conqueror"

I know, in You, I am a conqueror.
But sometimes, it's hard;
Hard to believe,
Hard to conquer,
Especially when I don't feel strong.

Oh, how I wish I could be more courageous.
I still worry relentlessly about many things.
From past and future circumstances.

Could you remind me today,
To be strong and brave ?
Could you send your Spirit to remind me,
That I am a conqueror.
For when I'm with You,
I can conquer everything.

"Surrender"

You are not alone.
You never were.
You never will be.

Surrender your heart today,
To those who deserve it.

Keep your strength.
Keep your name unchanged.

Surrender your gifts that help you,
Ease your anxious spirit
And keep your confidence too.

What you are,
Who you are,
Is of no price.

All you oughtta do, is surrender,
To the open arms of Christ.

"Bam"

Bam.
You have power to fight the lies.
Bam.
You have the power to not compromise.

Bam.
You have the power to live in truth.
Bam.
You have the power to do what is right to do.

"Clarity"

Listen to your mind
Throw out the whispering words.
Pour out your love to others freely,
Shine your pure light all over humanity.

"12 Days of Hell"

On the first day you're selfish.
I think that I can change it.

On the second day, you're jaded.
Making me feel uncalled for shame.

On the third day, you lie to look sharp.
With a little gaslight- leaving me in the dark.

On the fourth day, you make no room.
Some sort of way to act all superior too.

On the fifth day you prove to be unfaithful.
Then play the victim all way through.

On the sixth day I pretend I can take more;
Of your toxicity seeping at the core.

On the seventh day, the evil doesn't rest.
Hence, you continue to put me to the test.

On the eighth day, your harsh words have deviated;
Starving my need to ever feel appreciated.

On the ninth day, you spread the word that I've
lost my mind;
All because I stood up to you for ONE time.

On the tenth day, my heart feels like broken glass.
A mind restless and my spirit aghast.

On the eleventh day, you smile while you watch
me bleed.
I guess my brokenness is what you feed.

On the twelfth day, I finally run from your
daily attack:
Your power to hurt me is gone,
And will never come back.

"Anxiety"

My anxious heart is weighing me down today.
I confess that I have become consumed:
By my own thoughts,
Insecurities and doubts,
All spiralling:
Into old and made- up issues.

I have truly lost sight of who I am,
As well as who You are.
I have truly lost sight on how to begin again,
As much as how to speak my mind.

Clearly, anxiety for me, doesn't just 'kick in',
Rather it makes itself quite comfortable,
Clearly, anxiety for me, seems endless,
Taking away my days with a smile.

"Cut the Cord"

Fools take a knife and stab the wise in the back.
So, the wise take the knife,
Cut the cord,
And free themselves from the fools.

"It Sickens Me"

It sickens me that there are people who can,
Make up so many lies to against a fellow man.

It sickens me that there are people who,
Spread rumours and destroy innocent
people through.

It sickens me that this world normalises that
Jealous as well as envy,
Will come from people who are sad.

It sickens me that the people would rather consider
The lies and deception that makes a saint,
Look like, a strange, hard-core sinner.

"Beautiful Fragrance"

Beautiful Fragrance.
You are worthy of honour.
You are worthy of praise.

Beautiful Fragrance.
You are sweet as a flower.
You are compassionate to all, without shame.

Beautiful Fragrance.
You are present in all ways of life.
You are loving and strong at the same time.

Beautiful Fragrance.
You are crushed by the sword that fell.
To resurrect each person's broken shell.

"Beauty of Silence"

Revel in the beauty of your soul's peace and quiet.
Recognize three noises to avoid in your daily life.

"Boundary"

B is for being aware.
O is for being aware of what is and is not.
U is for unacceptable.
N is for normalising the times you say no.
D is for doing what you know is best for you.
A is for appreciating and accepting yourself.
R is for responsibility in making your own choices.
Y is for looking after yourself first, before
serving others.

" Desire"

I desire Your peace to rule in my heart.
When I feel uneasy or unsettled,
I want to know You are near to me.
I desire Your love to rule my life always.
When I feel fearful and down,
I want to know You'll settle my spirit.

"Always Good"

Today, I have the strength to see good.
Tomorrow, I have the good to flow what I do.
So, today, tomorrow and forever, I'll be sure to;
Thank my good family and friends carry me through.

"Hard Days"

On the hard days, help me to remember you.
For You are never far away.
Your strength is always fighting for me.
I need only to be still.

Day 103/365

"People are Like Books"

People are like books.
Some people deceive you with their covers.
Some people surprise you with their content.

" Masterpiece"

For we are God's masterpiece.

" I Will Be With You"

When you walk through the waters,
I will be with you.
When you pass through the rivers,
I will be with you.
When you walk through the fire,
I will be with you.
When you pass through the desert,
I will be with you.

" Equipped"

You are called for a reason.
The gift of salvation is always in season.
You are His workmanship, created good.
You are safe to fulfil your calling too.

Stop avoiding yourself and purpose.
Stop chasing your tail.
Trust in the good to prevail.
Time after time.

You are equipped for getting the job done.
You are equipped to experience matchless joy,
From now on.

"Focus"

Focus.
Do not depend on your own thoughts,
Ideas or understanding.

Focus.
Live out your designed calling,
Stand your ground and stop stalling.

"Someone like You Should"

Someone like you should:
Create a world of kindness being the 'in' fashion for
every year.

Someone like you should:
Normalise honesty that surpasses all understanding.

Someone like you should:
Surprise the people with love that overflows
the brim.

Someone like you should:
Write a book where the main character slowly falls in
love with the reader.

Someone like you should:
Give hope to the forgotten ones, starving for a
righteous leader.

"Wait"

Wait.
You will be exalted.
Wait.
You will have mercy.
Wait.
You will see justice.
Wait.
You will taste grace.
Wait.
Blessed is the one who waits.

Day 110/365

"Love"

Love every person with genuine affection. Love with delight for the close and far brethren.

"Nothing"

Nothing can defeat you without your consent.

Day 112/365

"Smile"

To someone not smiling today.

Be sure to give a smile their way.

"Deer Lesson"

The deer is better than the lion.
The lion runs for perishing food and vain control.
Whereas the deer runs for its life.
A deer runs for a purpose.
Why aren't you?

"Calm Confidence"

Your presence is the joy of my life.
You will not abandon the poor,
You will not abandon the needy.
You will help and bless all that call onto You;
Your love gives me calm confidence.

"Evil People"

Evil people seem to experience success.
Evil people actively seek out those who are poor,
helpless, or weak to take advantage of them.
Rather than being ashamed of such actions,
The evil people brag about them.
For that very reason,
It can sometimes seem that God does not exist.
Such a thought brings out sense of frustration
and anguish.
In contrast, you and I should know that God is aware.
He is not asleep.
What God has accomplished for us before, now and in
the future,
Is enough to preserve our confidence.

"Struggle, Observe, Trust"

Struggle.
Triumph over a strong temptation.
Observe.
Protect your innocence.
Trust.
Keep your ground.

"Joy"

Let all that talk with you rejoice.
Let them sing joyful praises forever.
Spread your joy on your fellow men.
May all those that know and love you,
Carry the joy you have always.

"What would a Dog Do? "

In every situation ask yourself "What would
a Dog do?"

So, if you cannot eat or play with a situation that
stresses you out;
Do what a dog would -pee on it (situation) and bark
it out.

"Agreeable Friends"

Animals ask no questions,
Animals pass no criticisms.
That is why animals are better than most,
As well as such agreeable friends.

"Average"

The average animal,
Whether small or large;
Is nicer than an average person's heart.

" Rise"

The more clutter and noise you let go, the higher you
will rise.

" Sing, Love, Dance and Live"

Sing from the top of your lungs,
Like there is no one listening.

Love deeply with no fear,
Like you have never been hurt.

Dance openly as if you're a swan,
With no worry that someone's watching.

Live freely and simply in every way,
Creating a slice of heaven on earth.

"Your Life is Like a Movie"

When you are feeling undeniably sad,
You are living a soap opera and drama.

At the times you are feeling angry,
You are living a live action party.

During the instances where you find yourself afraid,
You are living in suspense all the way.

Finally, when you look at yourself in the mirror,
every day,
You are living a horror slash paranormal sort of day.

Now, dear reader if that horror joke (despite lame)
made you smile,
Then you are living a comedy: the spice of life that
must be on replay.

"I'll be Coming 'Round the Mountain When Gandalf Comes"

When I turned eight years old, I failed to find a wardrobe. Not just any wardrobe that you see in a mundane house. But a magical wardrobe that would take me to a whole new world, like it did for Lucy Pevensie. Narnia.

When I turned eleven years old, I was disappointed to not receive a letter. Not just any letter that you get in a mundane mailbox. But a magical letter delivered from an owl named Hedwig. A letter that would give me a purpose in this life, as it did for Harry potter. Hogwarts.

When I turned twelve years old, I was left alone as my satyr did not show up. Not just any satyr that you read about in mundane fairy-tale books. But a magical satyr that would challenge me, like he did for Percy Jackson. Camp Half-Blood.

Now, I am not yet fifty years old. Yet, when I am graced to reach that ripe age; be sure to know that I'll be coming 'round the mountain for one. The one being- Gandalf the Grey, to take me on an adventure, as he did for Bilbo Baggins. The Lord of the Rings.

"Don't Tell Me"

Don't tell me what people gossiped about me
in person.
Don't tell me what rumours you heard by phone call.
Just tell me why such small people were comfortable,
To talking badly about me, to you...
That is all.

"Flee Like a Bird"

Flee like a bird from the mountains.
Run away from a place, or situation of danger.

Flee like a bird from the waterfalls.
Keep people guessing, what you're all about.

Flee like a bird from the deserts.
Find meaning in the loneliness, you sometimes feel.

Flee like a bird from the hailstorms,
Rest assured your secret hurt, will soon heal.

" To be"

To be good.
To be pure.
To be kind.
Be prepared.
To be tested.
Thoroughly.
At all times.

" See it All"

See it all.
See the true world around you.
Be the light of your own life.
See how you can learn how to be;
Content with what happens in sight.

See it all.
Be of the world, but not in the world.
See and remember the right way.
For you are made for so much more-every day.

"Sananos" by Marcos Witt

We are your people, and today we humble ourselves
before you.
We are your people, in need of You.
We have sinned, we have left your way, your truth.
We humble ourselves; our Earth heals today.

Heal us! heal us!
It is the cry of this people, humbled before You.
Save us! save us!
It is the prayer of your children, prostrate before You.
Heal us, heal us.
Heal us, heal us.
We are your children, we recognize our pride,
our mistake.
We are your children; we ask you today for
forgiveness.

"Thunderstorms"

Thunderstorms are a great manifestation of warmth,
And at the same time, can be terrifying to watch.

Thunderstorms are inclusive of wind, water,
and light,
And at the same time, can disrupt your sleep at night.

Thunderstorms are brilliant for they are
nature's proof;
That screaming out loud (sometimes) does
some good.

"Coffee Pun"

Coffee has a rough time in my house; for every morning it gets mugged.

Day 132/365

"Tortilla Pun"

I've written a song about tortillas. Scratch that. It is more of a rap.

Day 133/365

"Right and Left"

Make sure you give your loved ones the right time.
Not what is left.

"Donut Pun"

Live your life like a donut. Look at the donut in every situation. Not the hole.

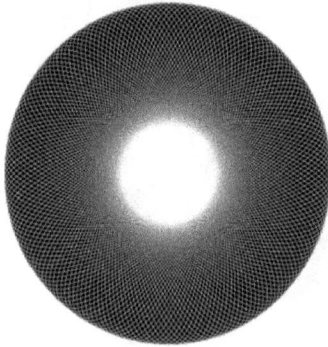

"Pea Pun"

Happea-ness is beaning together- not disconnected.

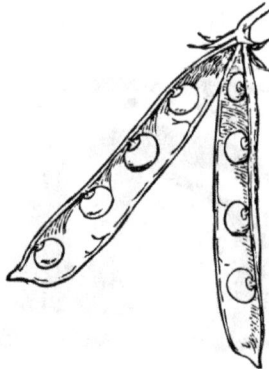

" Leaf Pun"

Be-leaf in yourself today and always.

"Cake Pun"

There are those who only dream or talk about cake.
Then there are those who bake it to happen.
Be the latter.

"Fruit Pun"

If you were a piece of fruit, you would be a fine-apple.
Never forget that.
For you are truly one in a melon,
And a berry special human!

"Bee Pun"

Always be yourself.
Remember that what is meant to be, will be.
Be positive.
Be sweet as can be.
Do your own sting!

" Listen"

Listen to what people don't say.

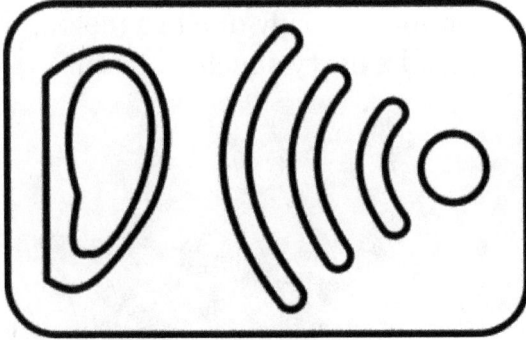

"Be True"

Be true as true can be. The world can adjust.

"Failure"

Your failure is not the antonym of success. Your failure is part of the success to come.

"Sunshine, Freedom, Flower"

It is not enough to just live.
It is not enough to just exist.
You deserve the light from sunshine.
You deserve the taste of true freedom.
And you deserve a flower of courage to make it count.

"Best Views"

The best views always come from the hardest climbs.

"If You Want to Succeed"

Every day is an opportunity to change for the better. So, if you want to succeed, focus on changing yourself.

"Plan?"

You don't always need a plan.
Hell, sometimes you have a plan and it doesn't
go through.
So, what do you do?
Well, sometimes all you can do is breathe.
Breathe, trust the process, and let go.
For what is meant to happen for you,
Will happen for you.
Regardless of what you plan to do.

"Small Steps"

The most incredible journeys you will go through, all begin with intentional small steps.

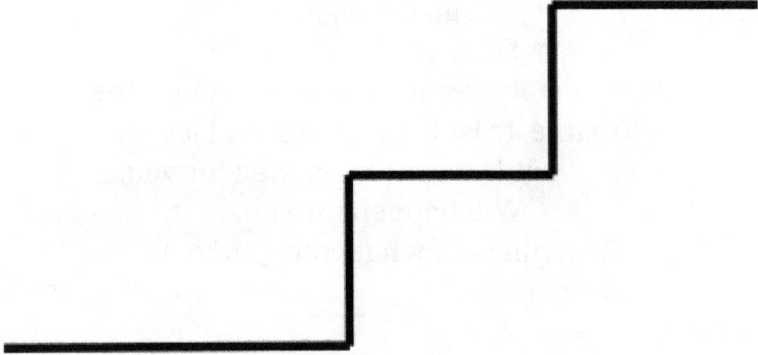

Day 148/365

" Shine Brighter"

The sky is filled with stars every night.
Take that as your personal reminder,
There is always room to shine brighter.

"Things to Remember"

1. Tomorrow is a new day.

2. Making mistakes is part of life.

3. Saying 'no' is okay.

4. Not everyone has to like you.

5. Beauty and strength comes from within.

"Project : You"

You are the greatest project you will ever work on.

Day 151/365

"Butterfly"

Just like the caterpillar who thought that the world was ending before it turned into a butterfly; you too will find your butterfly moment soon.

" Great Changes"

All great changes in your life, will be preceded
with chaos.

"Silence is Golden"

Your meaningful silence is always better than your
meaningless words.

"Leader"

Be intelligent, honest, and creative too.
Be a confident, driven, and courageous mood.
Be a leader,
But not in a material sense.
Yes, be a humble leader,
Edifying your family and friends.

"Promises"

The Lord's promises for you are pure, like silver refined in a furnace, purified seven times over. He will bless and protect you in everything you do. All you must do is trust in His promises made specifically for you.

"Keep and Apply"

Keep numbers on your days.
Apply goodness in your heart.
Keep focused on the good fight.
Apply wisdom from the start.

"Stop"

Stop feeding your inner demons.
And stop playing back your mistakes.
Stop carrying the list of mishaps.
And stop beating yourself on your state.
Stop doubting what God has already forgiven.
And stop nit picking the harm already done.
Stop thinking that you are not worthy.
And stop forgetting your number One.

"Your Unfailing Love"

I trust in Your unfailing love.
You make me rejoice always.

I trust in your plan of salvation.
Your goodness moves me to praise.

"You are Loved"

Above all, remember how much you are loved.
You are loved with great sincerity.
You are loved for serendipity.
You are loved, with an everlasting love.

"Brave and Courageous"

Here is what I've learnt from this time.
Do not give up.
Do not fall into despair because you're impatient.
Always hold onto the hope you carry.
Keep being brave and courageous enough,
To make what you truly want.

"8 Steps to Heaven"

Walk blamelessly.
Speak the truth from your heart.
Live righteously.
Don't use your tongue to slander or harm.
Do no evil to your neighbour.
Speak no evil, see no evil and be no evil too.
Honour those who love the Lord.
Serve the people, with no further ado.

"Kindness Coat"

The most fashionable coat is a coat of kindness. Wear it wherever and whenever you want. Then be sure to wash the coat thoroughly with incredible love.

Day 163/365

" He Will Always"

He will always be with you.
He will always listen to you.
He will always love you.

"To Do Shift"

Choose kindness. Always.
Let go of what you can't control to change
what you can.
Count your blessings, not the calories you take.
Listen to the Spirit inside you.
Walk humbly in every place you go.
Live like you are a stranger in this world.
Show love to all, like you've never been hurt.

"Truth Be Told"

Words are free.
It's the way you use words that will cost you.
So, the best thing to do with your words, it to say the truth.
For when you say the truth, you'll never have to remember what you said.

"Inspire"

Inspire people.
Be the reason that people look forward to
another day.
Inspire people.
Make a difference to someone's life today.

"Words"

Your words can create.
Your words can destroy.
So, choose your words wisely,
And be sure to talk nicely.

"Travelling will Make You SANE"

S stands for South America.
A stands for Australia, Asia, Africa, and
Antarctica too.
N stands for North America.
E stands for Europe through.
As this acronym for all the world, equates brilliantly
in this way.
Truth can be told that travelling, really does
make one SANE.

"Back to You"

All the love you have given to the wrong people, will
find its way back to you.

Day 170/365

"Goodness"

Life has taught us that it costs nothing to be kind.
So be sure to sprinkle goodness to others, all
the time.

"Footprints"

Leave footprints of love and kindness
wherever you go.

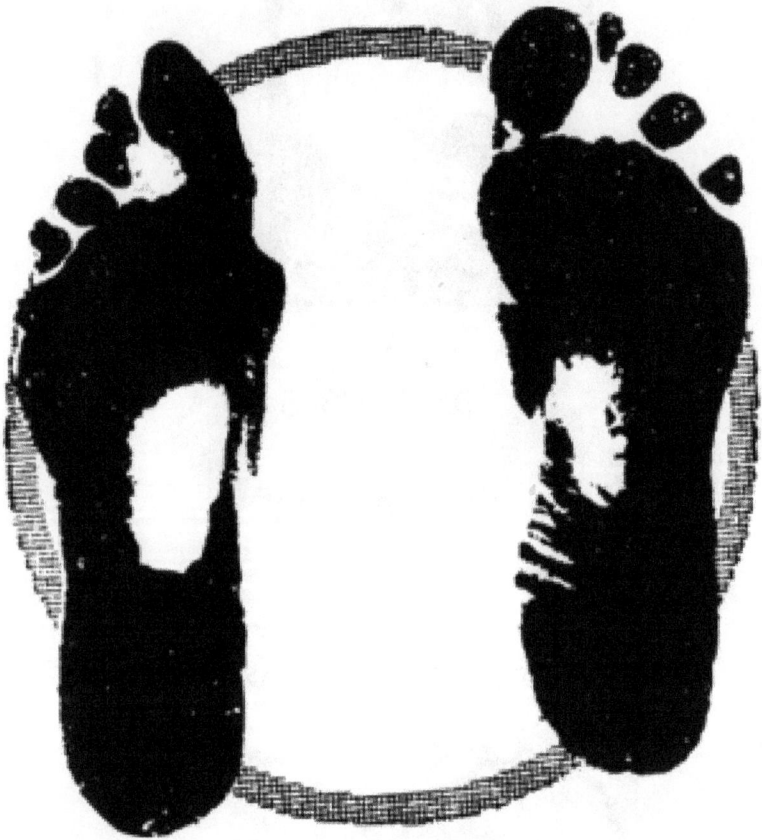

"Kindness" by Henry Wadsworth Longfellow

Kind hearts are the gardens, kind thoughts are
the roots.
Kind words are the flowers, kind deeds are the fruits.
Take care of your garden today and every day.
And be sure to pluck out the weeds.
Fill your garden only with sunshine,
Kind words and kind deeds.

"Kindness" by Amelia Earhart

A single act of kindness throws out roots at all directions, and the roots spring up into new trees.

"Enough"

Remind yourself today that you do enough, have enough, and are enough.

"Stay Positive" inspired by Pope Kyrillos IV

Stay positive.
For there are no such thing as a bad or good day.
There are only days where we do intentionally well.
And days where we could've done better if we'd
just pray.

"You Can"

Do all the good you can.
Use all the means you can.
In all the ways you can.
In all the places you can.
At all the times you can.
To all the people you can.

"Mistake"

Never make the same mistake twice. But make it
seven times to just be sure.

"Human Logic"

We cut down the trees for paper.
Then we use paper to spread awareness of
climate issues;
From global warming, overfishing,
To the oxygen reduction from cutting down too
many trees.

"Deliverance"

Know from the wider testimony,
That You are promised deliverance.
Stay spiritual in the present,
While being spiritual and bodily in the age to come.

Know that common grace in this world,
Is available for all always.
Stay patient in all bodily healing,
While being strong in spirit.

Know that you have big plans for this world,
And they are all secure.
Stay hopeful with a wing of security.
Even amidst this world's uncertainties and sufferings.

"Tell me Little Lamb"

Tell me little lamb,
What do you see or feel,
When you hear His voice speaking?

Tell me little lamb
Is it life or in death,
That He is worthy of our trust and respect?

Tell me little lamb
How did it feel to be lavishly embraced too,
By a Man and King, who loves you?

" Contractions Everywhere"

I just realised that 'never' is the contraction of
'not ever'.
Also, that 'blush' is the contraction of 'blood rush'.
And that studying is the contraction of
'student dying'.
No wonder why hardly any person enjoys studying.
Funny how contractions work, huh?

" Regulate"

Regulate.
Regulate your emotions today.
Regulate your emotions to manage all pain:
From the pain of others that manipulate,
To the pain of situations that you hate.

Regulate.
Regulate your emotions tomorrow.
Do not be a slave to your emotions,
Or you will be find many sorrows.

Regulate.
Regulate your emotions from now onwards.
Attain the freedom from controlling your emotions.
A freedom based on truth that lifts you upwards.

Day 183/ 365

"Advice"

Instead of giving advice or "your two cents".
Focus on being a good listener to your dear friends.

Day 184/ 365

"Death"

When faced with the death of a loved one,
please know,
That you mustn't apologise for not wanting to show.
No one should expect you to just quickly move on.
No one should push you to be a shoulder to cry on.
Your grieving has no expiry date.
So, take your time, for goodness' sake!

"Gut"

Trust your humble gut instinct,
As it's connected to your wonderful brain.
Be sure to follow that gut instinct tugging,
For often than not,
It'll end up keeping you sound and safe.

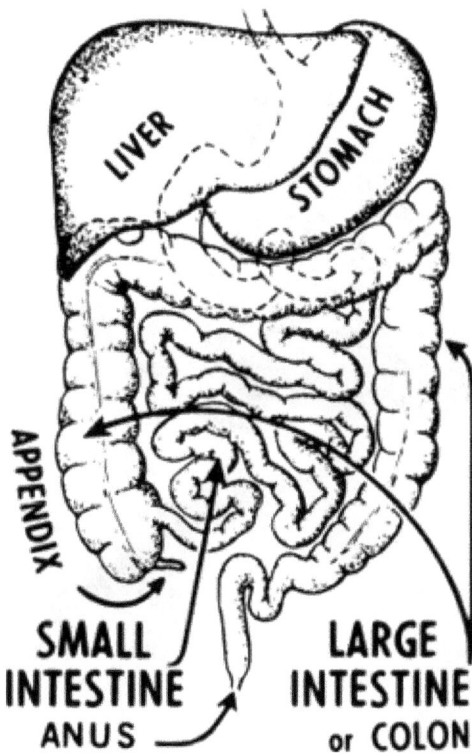

"Say Anything"

Stop letting meaningless words to bring you down.
People too often talk and say nonsense.
So be sure to not join this notoriously popular club ;
And rather, choose to use your words for common
sense and love.

"Just Because"

Just because you can, doesn't mean you should.

"Sit in the Car"

Sit in the car and finish listening to that song.

"Declutter"

Declutter your life.
Donate and give.
Declutter your life,
Take only the good,
And leave the shid.
For as everything, looks better when it's clean,
Your heart and soul will look better,
When you take care of it, intentionally.

"Stories"

Our stories are filled with broken pieces.
Terrible choices and ugly truths.
But our stories are also filled with wonderful things;
From major comebacks, peace,
And unlimited grace that moves.

"You've Changed"

"You've changed" the naysayers go.
At that you must respond: "Yes, I've changed. How
about you?".

For when you remove the people who toxify and
manipulate,
You can invest in self-development with no
interest rate.

So, next time a person crossly states how
you've changed;
Be sure to thank them first, before you bid
them good day!

"Just Like That"

One day, just like that, you'll find:
A re-discovered frame of mind.

Yes, just like that,
Your light will return back.
Making you ready for anything,
Even the little set-backs.

Indeed, just like that,
You'll take back your power,
For you are a warrior now,
And the victor of this very hour.

"Good Hearts"

It's time for people with good hearts- YOU, to win.

"Lamenting"

Life goes on.
You always have a choice.
Do not lament,
About your career, objects,
Or if your plans will turn out.
Your worth more than a career.
Your worth more than objects.
Your plans can change.
You have a life.
Live it well.

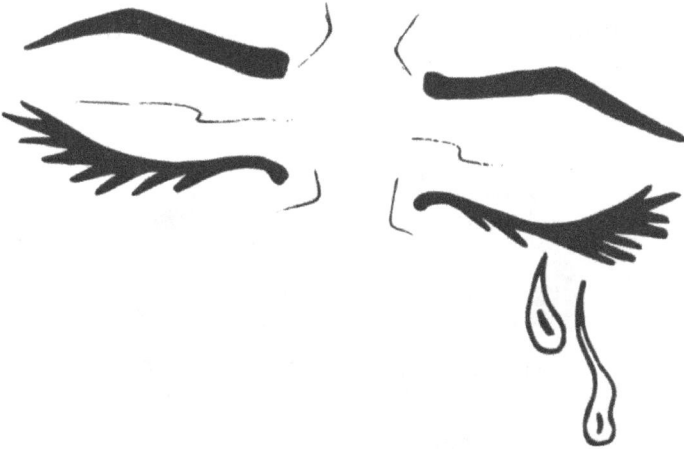

"Guard Your Heart"

Your problem is not poor intellect,
Or a lack of evidence and trying.
Your problem is to leave your heart unguarded,
Time after time.

This world is not perfect,
Never was and will never be.
Hence, stop allowing corruption
And ruin, enter your heart, so quickly.

From an eternal and holy perspective,
You are in this human race to succeed.
Thus, do not rush, take your own time;
Be good to yourself and to others, intentionally.

"Life is Good"

Life is good when you don't judge people's choices every day.
Life is good when you are thankful for what you have.
Life is good when you spend your time in giving love.
Life is good when you decide to make it that way.

"Keep Me Safe"

Keep me safe.
I have come to you for refuge.
Every good thing comes from you;
The good people are my heroes too.

Keep me safe.
For I take pleasure in doing what is right.
You alone are my inheritance.
You alone have taught me how to sacrifice.

Keep me safe.
Guard all that is rightfully mine.
The land given to me is pleasant.
You are my greatest spirit guide.

Keep me safe.
Make my heart glad and rest.
For as I know for sure once more,
Your love for me, has no end.

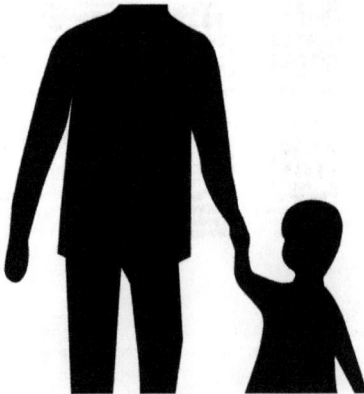

" Apple of the Eye"

Keep me as the apple of your eye.
Ask to keep your eyes on me and not lose sight.
I will regard you as one would a cherished child.
I will regard you just as a mother bird protects
her young.
I will regard you like the shepherd David was
by the Lord.

Keep me as the apple of your eye.
Be confident that you shall see wonders too.
You deserve a great love that nourishes,
Encourages and makes you feel brand new.

Keep me as the apple of your eye.
Stay vindicated by the enemies that are found.
Yet, rest assured that in every circumstance,
you will find
Help from your friends, and the strangers around.

"The Heavens are Telling"

The Heavens are telling the glory of God,
The wonder of His work displays the firmament.
Today declares a new start,
So, remember to seize it.

The Heavens are telling the glory of God,
The wonder of his work displays the firmament.
In all the lands resounds the word,
Never unperceived, ever understood it.

The Heavens are telling the glory of God,
The wonder of His work displays the firmament.
Your story begun from when you were just a cell,
So, be sure to rejoice always in it.

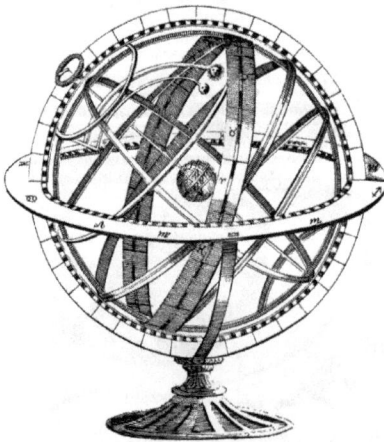

"Talk"

Some people talk too much.
Some people talk too little.
So be sure to find and apply the 'goldilocks balance',
For whenever you talk with people.

Day 201/365

" Stop Talking"

When you have stopped talking to me, be sure to stop
talking about me too.

"Buddha Wisdom"

See no evil.
Hear no evil.
Do no evil.
Be no evil.

Day 203/365

" Crying"

Crying is a way your eyes speak when the mouth cannot express how much your heart is broken.

"Remember"

Remember, if someone talks about a problem they have with you, they can always call you. But if they do not have your number or even try to get it, then you can remember the truth. For truth be told. The truth is rarely told. Yet, remember that the truth is that the person never knew you well enough to have a problem. Remember this my friend. And don't let any fool keep you from finishing first place.

"My Steps"

My steps have held to Your path.
My feet will not stumble.

My steps have taken me to Your shield.
My feet will remain grounded.

My steps have lifted my head up high.
My feet will carry my purpose.

"Generosity"

See how your generosity can help people gain faith in humanity.

Day 207/365

"Apology"

Your apology needs to be loud as your disrespect was.

"Potterhead Lessons"

Voldemort: The one who died drunk in power.

Professor Snape: The one who died for love.

Professor Dumbledore: The one who cared for the greater good.

Lily Potter: The one who died for her family.

James Potter: The one who died for his family.

Harry Potter: The one who greeted death as an old-time friend.

Ron Weasley: The one who persevered until the very end.

Hermione Granger: The one who sacrificed a lot for her friends.

You: The one who is brilliant; and destined for fulfilling all dreams, unto the end.

"Boy Meets Rabbit"

One day, a long time ago,
A Boy was allowed,
To walk home all alone.
With no parent about.

As he walked for a while,
The Boy got tired and scared.
Before greeting a Rabbit that cared.

So the Rabbit and Boy conversed for a while.
The Rabbit taught the Boy interesting things,
As well as jokes that made him smile.

"How strange that the grass is all that remains after
the storm?", stated the Boy, before he instantly left.

"Sometimes being soft, is strong", the Rabbit
silently said.

"Love, in All its Glory"

Once upon a time, all feelings and emotions went on
a retreat.
The retreat was a chance for them to finally greet.
According to their nature, each was having a
unique moment.
Before a storm impeded, with no sufficient notice.

As the announcement caused a sudden panic.
All feelings and emotions ran to the boats, in havoc.
The boats, even those damaged, were used to depart.
Ensuring the feelings and emotions weren't apart.

Love was growing restless and dejected.
Just then someone called out: "Come Love, be
protected!"
Love did not know who was being so kind,
Before jumping on the last boat in time.

After witnessing that scene, Knowledge said
with a smile,
"Oh, that was Time. Love truly takes a while".

Love then asked out loud, the following:
'Why would Time stop to pick me up in the
morning?"
Knowledge responded with no shadow of doubt:
"It's because Time knows your true greatness inside
and out".

The most important messages that can be learned
from this story.
Is that with time, we can realize the value of love, in
all its' glory.

"Love Deeply"

Love each other deeply as mothers and fathers.
Love each other deeply as daughters and sons.
Love each other deeply as brothers and sisters.
Love each other deeply as yourself- number one.

"Strengthened"

As He stood by me, and strengthened me, I could
climb the mountain.
You are always reliable, my strength and defence.
I have nothing to fear because you are with me.
You protect me.
Your promises are always secure.
You are my strength.
And through me being strengthened, the message
was proclaimed:
To the naysayers and doubters, I am strengthened to
defeat a lion, and be saved.

"Rest"

Why are you desperately active and in fear of rest?
Since when did burn out, make us be the best?

Now, my friend,
I challenge you to work.
Without fuss like before.
Remain confident in yourself.
Shine bright from within.
Then take absolute rest- truest way to win.

"Promise Yourself"

To be strong in mind that nothing and no one, can disturb your peace.

To live in the faith and hope that the whole world is better with you in it.

To apply a full- time reflection to better yourself- not casually criticise others.

To be just as enthusiastic about the success of others as your own.

To remind all your family and friends of their value in your life.

To think well of yourself and hold yourself accountable for greater things.

To forget the mistakes of your past, to move onwards and upwards.

To choose being brave over doing what is easily accepted.

"Guilty Until Proven Innocent"

As I travel in this time and space, I have learned to listen to my mother's intuitions about life and people. Not only that, but I have also learned to listen to her spin off on many sayings. For instance, you probably have heard the saying 'innocent until proven guilty'. However, for my mother, the saying is 'guilty until proven innocent'. And in such a day and age we all live in, I would say right on!

"Boiling Water"

Boiling water makes potatoes soft and the eggs hard. This simple cooking fact is an excellent reminder that it is not the circumstances that shape us, it is who we are in essence.

"How to find Joy"

Comparison is the thief of joy. Therefore, joy can only be found when you stop comparing yourself.

"Open Your Eyes"

Sweetheart, open your eyes.
You are not the words that caused you pain.
Or that number on the scale that you read.
You simply, beautifully, and wonderfully made.

Sweetheart, open your eyes.
Look deep in your soul.
Keep up the good fight.
Cherish the real you, once and for all.

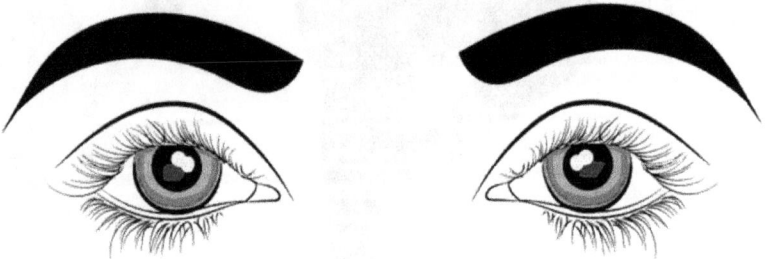

"Be Silent"

Be silent like deep water.

"Enjoy"

Yesterday is gone.
Tomorrow is never promised.
So, enjoy life TODAY.
Enjoy life amidst your problems.

"Strong"

You will never realise how strong you truly are; until being strong is your only choice.

"Be the Moon"

Everyone is preoccupied with being the sun to brighten somebody's life; but almost nobody wants to be the moon to light up somebody's darkness.

"Piano"

Life is like a piano. It has happiness- white keys.
It has sadness- black keys.
But as we go through life,
We learn that both,
White and black keys,
Make our lives a perfect symphony.

"Time Paradox"

We have not enough time to do things that we would like. Or have too much time spent on idleness- procrastination.

Day 225/365

"Words"

May there always be beauty in your words, and a feeling of calm in your silence.

Day 226/365

"Angel Wings"

My love, you went to Hell and came back with angel wings. And for that transformation, I'm so delighted in you.

Day 227/365

"Deep Question"

What is holding you back from pursuing what you really want?

"Anatomy Thought"

Have you ever considered how our hearts can sometimes be monstrous to our mental wellbeing? So, perhaps that's why our ribs are in a cage.

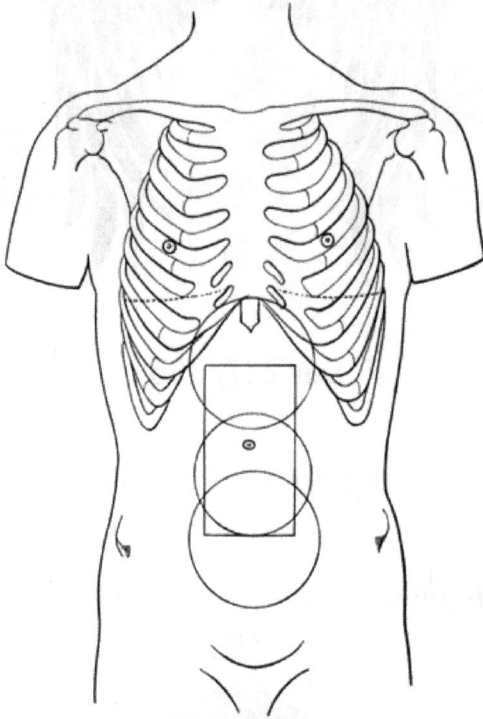

"Stay Blessed"

The things that you have been hoping and praying for, are coming your way. It will all fall into place at the time you least expect. Therefore, my friend, I challenge you to use this valuable time wisely, and stay blessed.

"Light and Darkness"

I will love Your light because it shows me the
narrow way.
I will love the darkness because it shows me
the stars.

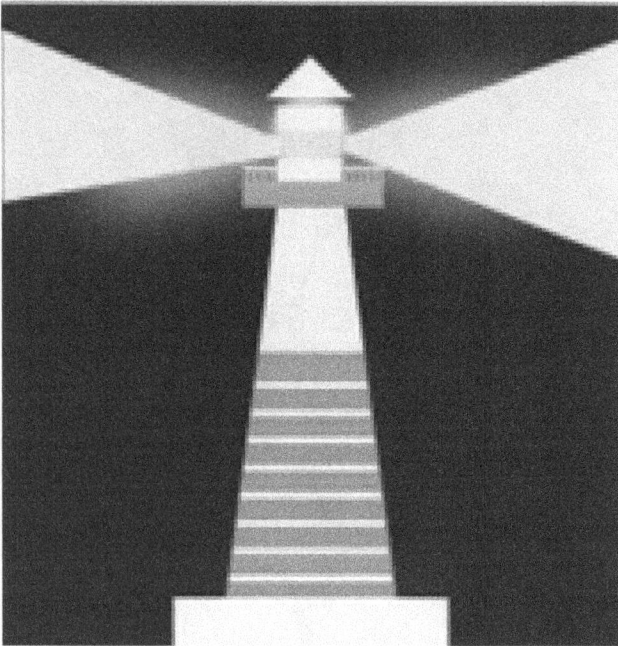

"Book"

I was only a mere chapter in your life story.
Not even a good one, if I may add.
So, the joke is on me.
As I had high hopes on our love never ending,
And made you the book in mine.

Day 232/365

"Sleep?"

Sleep will not help you if your soul is still tired.

Day 233/365

"Death"

No matter all our differences, one truth for
all remains:
That death imprinted on us all,
Yet kept quiet, on the total number of our days.

"Spiritual Blessings"

Your spiritual blessings are the greatest, most beautiful, and are completely yours.

Day 235/365

"Utmost Highest"

Be someone that can face things in the light of reality.
Be yourself. Always.

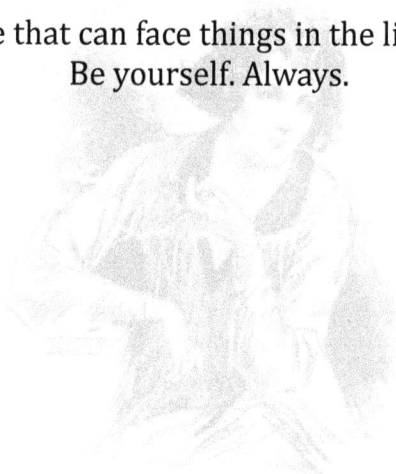

"Thank You"

Thank You for showing me mercy and kindness.
Thank You for being my healer, rescuer, and
comforter.
Thank You for always lighting up my world.
You make everything better than before.
So, for that I'll always say: thank you.
No one compares.
You are the best!

"Never Forget"

May I never forget the good things that you have
done for me.

"Desire and Purpose"

You will be granted according to your heart's desire
and be fulfilled in your purpose.

Day 239/365

"Lavish"

The banner that is over me,
Is full of love that has set me free.
You lavished Your love.
You lavish Your love,
On me.

"Joy"

Only when you acknowledge that the joy in the moment of victory comes from strength above; will you taste a kind of joy that lasts forevermore.

"Where are You Now?"

Where are You now?
I need you,
Right now in this moment.

Where are You now?
I am strong,
But my hope's slammed in.

Where are You now?
I have faith,
In You and Your promises.

Where are You now?
I will love,
Amidst all the torment.

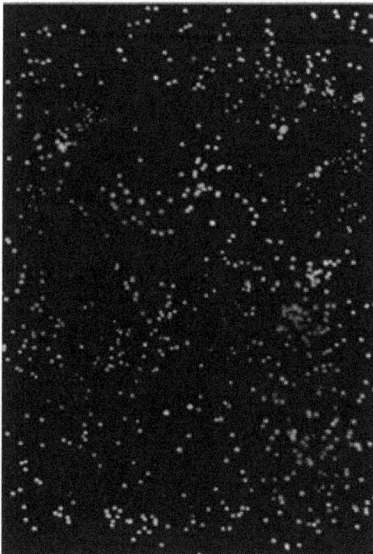

"Cinderella Goals"

Cinderella had her shoe fall off, albeit that she left shoe intentionally at the ball. For after her shoe was found by the prince, she was able to fit in the shoe perfectly; and thereby change her life forever. So, if Cinderella could make a better life for herself, you can too, boo.

Day 243/365

"Multitasking"

I can multitask so quickly.
For I can listen as much as ignore you,
As well as forget.

"Universe"

How exciting a thought that on one special day, the scientists will finally discover the centre of the universe. Alas, on that special day, such a discovery will baffle the people who thought that the universe revolved around 'them'.

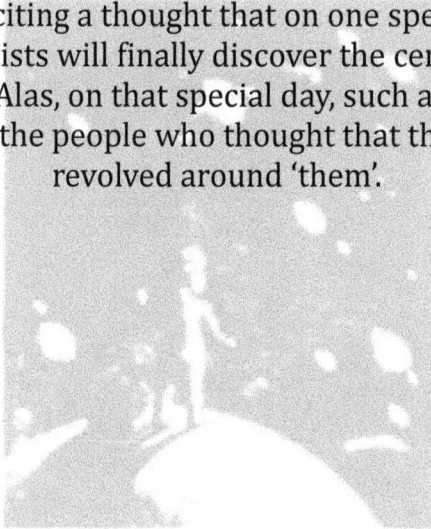

"Alphabet Letters"

Do not worry if your plan A failed. After all, there are 25 more letters in the alphabet for a reason.

"Talking to Yourself"

When I need expert advice, I talk to myself.

"Doormat"

If you don't like people stepping all over you, then get off the floor.

"Shame"

It is a shame that there are never enough hours in a day, to just hate everything.

"Relationships"

Relationships are a walk in the park- Jurassic Park.

"Embrace Your Mistakes"

My husband taught me to always embrace my
mistakes.
So, I make sure to hug him at least once, every day.

Day 251/365

"Coffee"

I love you more than coffee, but please don't make me
prove it.

"Quarantine"

Quarantine in 2020, taught me three things:

How to tell inside jokes with pun intended.
How to wear a mask inside and out.
How to cook with 'ready to eat meals' ordered online.

"Getting Anywhere"

The first step to getting anywhere in life, is to intentionally decide to not stay where you are.

Day 254/365

"Lifetime"

Give people the truth and they will think for a day. Give people a reason and they will think for a lifetime.

Day 255/365

"Awaken"

The more I feel awaken, the less I care to fit in.

"All My Days"

Why can't it be Monday, Tuesday, Saturday Sunday,
Wednesday, Thursday, Saturday, Sunday?

Day 257/365

" Far from Me"

Be not far from me.
When the trouble is near.
You are my only hope;
And I have none willing to help.

"Shadow of Death"

Even though I walk in the valley of the shadow of death, I will not fear any evil. For as the shadows are there, there must be light. Then, as You are light, I know You are with me. As You are with me in the shadows, I will stick with You, always.

"Create in Me"

Create in me a clean heart.
Renew a steadfast spirit within me.

Create in me a new set of eyes.
Open my mind to see what you see.

Create in me a brave stance.
Inspire me to take a chance.

Create in me a sweet melody.
Push me toward generosity.

Create in me an internal change.
Keep me in the narrow gate.

"My Hope is in You"

Show me Your ways.
Teach me Your paths.
Inspire me to speak- only when asked.
Guide me in the Truth.
Show me the way to Life.
Keep me strong in the faith.
Inspire me to never lose sight.
For my hope is in You.
Always.
Indeed.
My hope is in You.
From now,
Until eternity...

"Mistakes MythBusters"

Your mistakes are teachers, not attackers.
Your mistakes are just lessons, not lifetime losses.
Your mistakes are temporary detours, not the
destination.

"Lawyers and Judges"

We are often excellent lawyers for our own mistakes, even perhaps a loved ones' mistakes. Yet, at the same time, we're merciless judges over the mistakes of others, we unknowingly or knowingly, detest.

Day 263/365

"You are Everything I needed"

Isn't amazing that right now a person somewhere, in this very moment, even if a stranger, can quickly become the world to you?

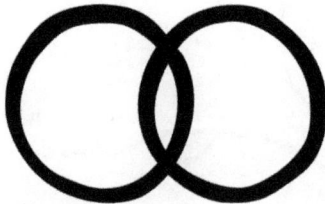

"I Love You"

You came into my life.
Unexpected.
I was praying for you.
Every night.
Now You're here.
I still can't comprehend it.

Even when I can't find the words.
To tell You.
How much You mean to me.
I want to show You.
With every look,
With every touch,
And every kiss.
That I wholeheartedly adore,
And love you!

"Keep it Real"

To truly 'keep it real', you must learn to accept your past, intently support your present, and boldly encourage your future.

"Green Flags"

Too often we read and see about 'red flags' to look out for. So, it's about time to remember the 'green flags' we are made to search for.
The green flags list, includes but are not limited to:
People who quickly reply; people who are messy; people who wear their hearts on their sleeves; people who text you to see you are safe; people who treat all with kindness; people who apologise for being difficult at times; people with a golden heart; people who give you grace; people who encourage you to reach for the sky; and people who are willing to openly communicate.

"Mind is Future"

If your mind is centred on injustices that you have received, you will soon become a bitter person indeed. But if your mind is centred on the blessings and mercy shown, you will attract joy wherever you go.

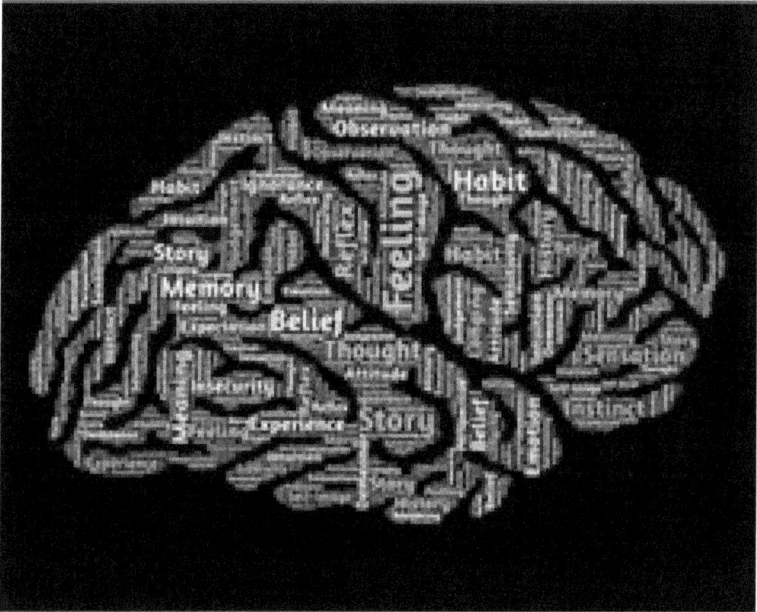

"Evil of Human Psyche"

Forgetfulness.
This is one of the evils of our human psyche.

Forgetfulness.
It makes us forget the good.
But dwell on the bad.

Forgetfulness.
Steers us to forget the compliments we take.
In place of comments that drown us in shame.

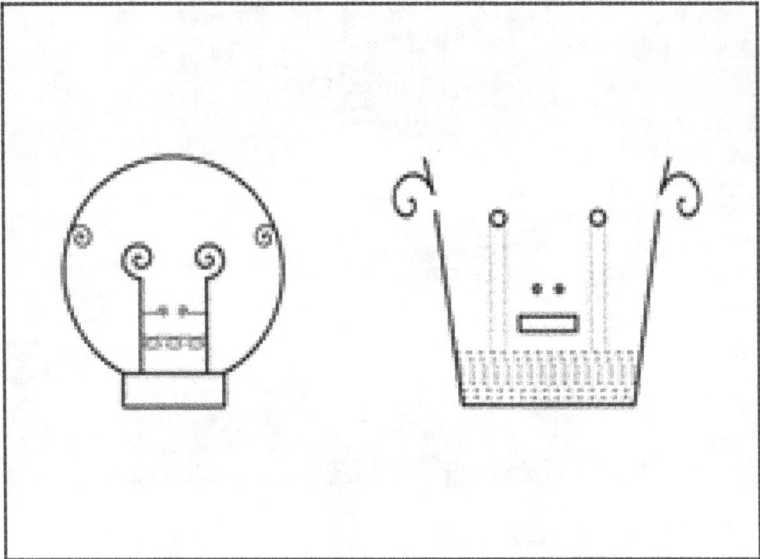

"East to West"

As far as the East is to the West, He has removed our
sins, one by one.
As far as the East is to the West, He has guided us
with light bright as the sun.
As far as the East is to the West, He removed all our
transgressions away.
As far as the East is to the West, He granted us
wonderful lessons for each day.
As far as the East is to the West, He showered us with
an abundance of love.
As far as the East is to the West, He guarded our
fragile souls and hearts.

"Faith"

To live by faith is to let Him take the lead. Your everyday walk is fuelled by faith, as it should be. So, do not forget, but remember that your faith is revived from simultaneously listening and doing, according to His will.

FAITH

"Good Father"

Thank You for being a Good Father.
I am so grateful and indebted to You.
Thank You for being my rock.
There is none I can rely always on, but You.
Thank You for giving me gifts,
Even what I forget to ask You for.
Thank You for blessing me abundantly.
Your light is a guide to keep me pure.
Thank You for being a Good Father,
I am so grateful and glad.
For before I was born, You formed me,
In the palm of Your hand.

"Don't Get Stuck"

Don't get stuck.
Move, travel, learn something new.
Take a risk in the madness.

Don't get stuck.
Shift and get out of your comfort zone.
Loosen up in pursuit of greatness.

Don't get stuck.
Walk closely with people you respect.
Keep courage as you stroll with intent.

"Last Long"

What comes easy will not last long.
What lasts long will not come easy.

Day 274/365

"Friedrich Nietzsche Quotable"

Whoever fights monsters should see to it that in the
process he does not become a monster. And if you
gaze long enough into an abyss, the abyss will gaze
back into you.

"Saint Augustine Quotable"

People go abroad to wonder at the heights of mountains, at the huge waves of the sea, at the long courses of the rivers, at the vast compass of the ocean, at the circular motions of the stars, and they pass by themselves without wondering.

"Loneliness"

Loneliness is tragic.
But not like sickness or loss.
Loneliness is tragic.
For no one is told how to cope.
Loneliness is tragic.
It is the thief of an outcast's hope.

"Lonely People"

I am lonely.
I am so lonely.
When will this mean loneliness fade away?
I am so lonely.
I am so very lonely.
When will this bitter loneliness stop today?

"Complicated Human"

I am a complicated human.
I like to be alone, but never lonely.
I don't like to stand out, but I'll never stoop down to
be a phony.

I am a complicated human.
I like to get what I get, yet still at times, end up upset.
I want a lot of space as much a kind person to face.

I am a complicated human.
I can forgive and yet vividly remember the
committed wrong.
I crave pure freedom as much as routines that last
long.

"Calories"

Calories are energy, not the enemy"

"Wisdom"

The wisdom we attain and apply, is from our healed pain in this life.

"Lovable"

Imagine growing up treated like you're unlovable.
To then realise that you were the worthiest.
Most lovable.
You were just surrounded by toxic people,
All of which used their self-hate,
To put out your light.
You are a light.
Always was.
Always will be.
This insight alone,
Should make you feel invincible.
Remember.
You are lovable.

"Greatest Wisdom"

The greatest wisdom in this life is kindness.

"Memory"

Nothing improves our memory than by trying to forget.

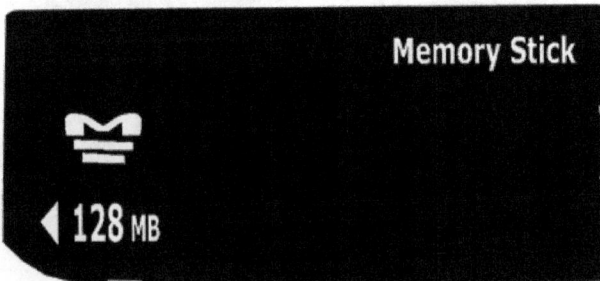

"Your Mind"

Whatever you carry in your mind now, can and will,
manifest.
If you continue to believe,
What you currently believe,
It will reflect in your actions.

And when you continue to act,
As what you have previously acted,
You will always achieve the same results.

But if you want a change.
Change of life and perspective.
You must change your mind,
With faith fuelled intention.

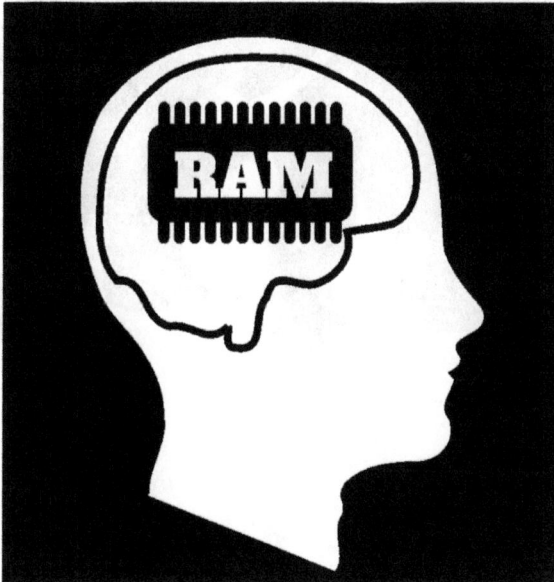

"The Wise"

The wise are not always silent, but they know exactly when to be.

"Is There?"

Without respect,
Can there be pure love?

Without pure love,
Are there other ways of communication?

Without ways of communication,
Is there a window to trust?

Without a window of trust,
Is there enough time to make it?

"Some Days"

Some days I wish I had the energy of a three-year-old, the body of a twenty-year-old, and the wisdom of a hundred-year-old.

"Life is Ironic"

Life is ironic.
It takes happiness from us,
To teach us what sadness is.
It makes noise,
To allow us to appreciate the silence.
It gives us people's absence,
To value people's presence.
Life is ironic.

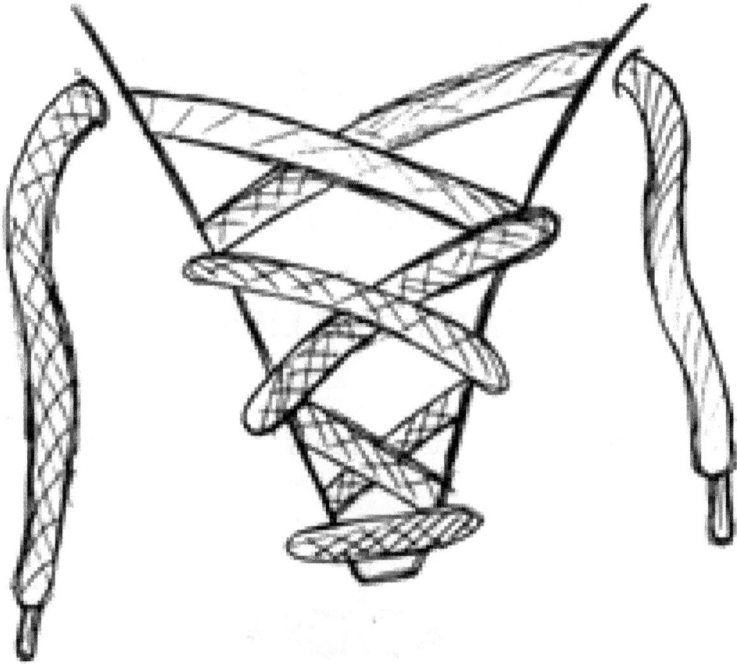

"Truth is Like a Lion"

The truth is like a lion, you don't have to defend it.
The truth will defend itself.
The truth will always come through.

Day 290/365

"Truth and Lies"

The truth is still truth, even if no one believes it.
The lies are still lies, even if everyone believes it.

"Government"

If you behaved openly like the government, you would be arrested.

"Fit in?"

If you do not fit in this society, then you can rest assured that you are doing the right thing.

"Stop Asking for Permission"

Stop asking for permission.
Channel Nike's slogan- 'just do it'.

"Yes, I am an Extremist"

Yes, I am an extremist.
I am an extremist for the acceptance of peace;
To the preservation of the good in humanity.

Yes, I am an extremist.
What is it to you?
I am an extremist against war,
To the divisions that violently seep through.

Yes, I am an extremist.
Now, why aren't you?
I am an extremist against the initiation of force.
To promoting the love of life, to take its course.

"She was Fragile"

She was fragile not like a leaf or flower.
She was fragile like a bomb.

"Apologies in Advance"

I would like to apologise in advance to those I have
not offended yet.
Please be patient with me.
I will get to you ASAP.

"We Travel"

We travel not to escape our scenery.
We travel not to escape our misery.
We travel not to escape from a 'hell'.
We travel to escape from ourselves.

"Success"

Success is not all on the same level, at the same time.
Afterall, a lion is still a lion, even when it is a cub.

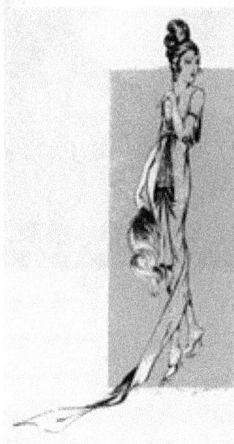

"Bad Company"

Just because you're lonely,
Doesn't mean you should accept bad friends.
As a person who is thirsty,
Doesn't drink poison,
In place of water given.
Do not deceive yourself.

For bad company,
Although satisfying to the body at the start,
Will artfully corrupt your soul and heart.

Day 300/365

"Challenge Accepted"

Challenges are what makes our lives interesting.
Overcoming them is what makes them meaningful.

"Not All"

Not all kings and queens wear crowns.
Not all heroes and heroines have capes.
Not all soldiers and warriors use swords.

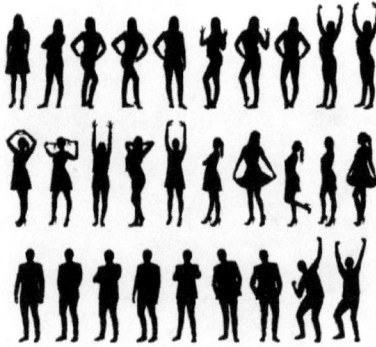

Day 302/365

"It's Best"

It's best to take refuge in You, and not fellow man.

"Peace"

Anything that costs your peace, is too expensive.

"Peace and Truth"

Try to keep the peace whenever possible.
But make sure to keep the truth at all rates.

"Friends and Enemies"

We may not like everyone,
And that is okay.
For we are taught to respect all,
Each day.

Although we may not be friends,
We're not enemies either.
I wish you, your daily bread,
Just not on my table either.

"I Choose You"

I choose You.
I will always choose You.
Without a shadow of doubt.
Over and over.
Until the day my heart stops beating,
Marking all my days over.
I will always keep choosing You.

"How to Love"

You taught me how to love, but not how to stop.

"You Were Born"

You were born to be perfect. For no one can perfectly
be you, except you.

"A Bad Generation"

Welcome to this bad generation:
Where the word loyalty is tattooed more than
practised.
Love is quoted rather than demonstrated.
And lying has become natural as saying the truth.

"Be a Donor"

Don't be a beggar for love.
Be a donor of love.

Don't be a beggar for kindness.
Be a donor of kindness.

Don't be a beggar for compassion.
Be a donor of compassion.

Don't be a beggar for peace.
Be a donor of peace.

Don't be a beggar for faith.
Be a donor of faith.

Don't be a beggar for joy.
Be a donor of joy.

Don't be a beggar for Him.
Be a donor of Him.

"Every Human"

Every human loves justice at another man's expense.
Every human loves the truth only when it makes
them look good.
Every human love grace when it is given to them.
Every human love modesty when they have
nothing to lose.

"Teach Me Your Paths"

I lift my soul to You.
In You, I place my trust.
Let me not to fall in shame.
Let not my enemies exult over me.

Many people want to put me to shame;
Many people want to be my enemy.
But I will not stand afraid.
For I know You are with me.

Lead me in Your Truth.
You're the essence of Truth in my heart.
I would wait for You, all day long.
I would cry for You, to hear my song.
Your mercies are countless,
Precious like a ruby gemstone.

Your paths have been from old.
So, teach me,
And keep me in them,
Forevermore.

"Integrity"

Vindicate me.
Vindicate me now.
What are you waiting for?
Vindicate me.
For I have walked to and fro,
From the East to the West,
Carrying my innocence.
Vindicate me.
Vindicate me and see.
That the person who you judge,
Has unwavering integrity.

do it right.

"Seeker"

We find it easy to trust in our wisdom, our
experience, our friends, and our resources too. But
we find it hard, albeit difficult, to even seek You.

"Oh Seeker"

Oh Seeker,
Forget your hunger and thirst.
Come see who gives healing from the hurt.

Oh Seeker,
Forget the past and future worries.
Come see who creates our steadfast path.

Oh Seeker,
If you trip or suffer on the road.
Remember for you, He died.

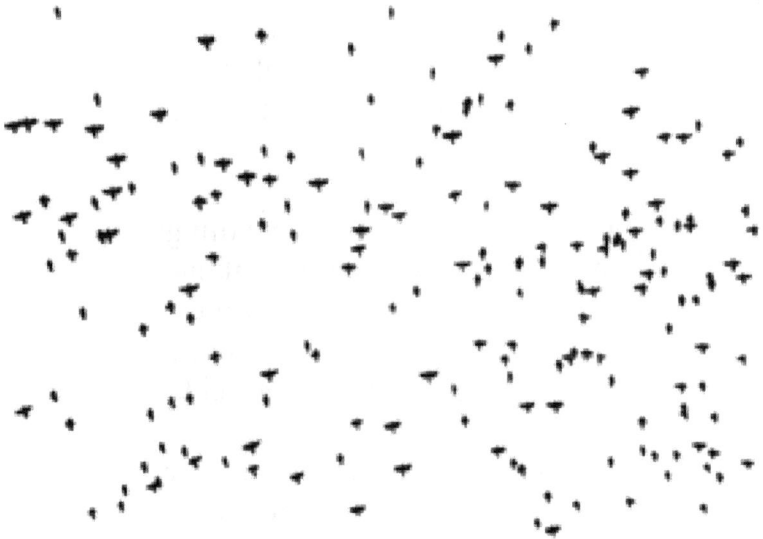

"A Stranger" by Pope Shenouda III

A stranger I lived in the world.
A foreigner like my forefathers.
A pilgrim in my attitude.
In my thoughts and my desires.

A stranger, I have no one to.
Unload on him, my thoughts so true.
The people do not like my roots.
Nor do they understand my end.
In craze arise the multitude.
In maddening noise without an end.
And I remain in solitude.
Serenity in my heart felt.

A stranger, I can find no home.
Nor a corner to rest alone.
I cast away the world's pleasures.
Ignoring her callings to me.

I went, I dragged away my things.
Away from their merry makings.
My heart silent, indifferent.
To all they think is important.
My listening will never yield.

To loud and worldly conversing.
I wander off all on my own.
So happy to be in the vast.
With my timbrel and my cymbal.
And melodies of praise I sing.

And now comes the holy moment.
In which I retreat with my King.
I roam about as a spirit.
Invisible to on-lookers.
The world alien I am to it.

A foreigner like my forefathers.
My existence is a triumph.
No wealth, power to disturb me.
No house is here to delay me.
Nor any friend or family.

And with me are sweet verses.
And great proverbs to console me.
The Bible here my only lamp.
And nothing else to concern me.

I do not know of any fear.
Nor any bonds that hinder me.
No longer does the world rule me.
Against me and at times for me.

I say to every enemy.
Who only wants to seduce me.
Beware that now I am alive.
A stranger as were my fathers.

"Trumpets"

The trumpets will be heard soon,
With happiness and sound of joy.
The trumpets will be heard soon,
With a great feast above the clouds.

"His Table"

Just for you,
He'll prepare a place on His table.
He's always waiting for you.
His heart is longing for you,
He always lives in You.
And you who live among the rocks.
Have no fears from all dangers.
His care for you is always stable,
As you sit at your place, on His table.

Day 319/365

"Kids Have Changed"

The old excuse 'kids have changed', contains no merit in my books. Parenting has changed. Society has changed. Technology has changed. The kids are innocent in this hot mess. First, parents work unholy hours to keep up with inflation rates and costs of living. Second, society continues to promote unhealthy expectations on what people should look and be like. Finally, technology continues to override the basics of relationship building.

Cue in when you tell me 'Kids have changed'. Well, here's the thing if you were a kid, what would you do? And if you answer that honestly, you'll too learn, that it's not their fault.

"King's House"

When the King's house burns down, he rebuilds it more beautiful.

"Answered Prayer"

To You, I call;
You are my Rock.
Please don't turn a deaf ear to me.
Hear my cry.
Be near as can be.
I call to You for help.
I lift my hands toward You. our Most Holy Place.
Do not drag me away with the wicked.
Or with those who do evil too.

I need an escape;
From people who harbour malice in their hearts,
Along with callous acts in all parts.
Can You please repay them for their deeds,
Against innocent people, and me?

Praise be to You alone.
For You have heard my cry.
You alone are my strength and my shield.
In You alone, can my spirit yield.
You alone are my answered prayer,
And I long to worship You.

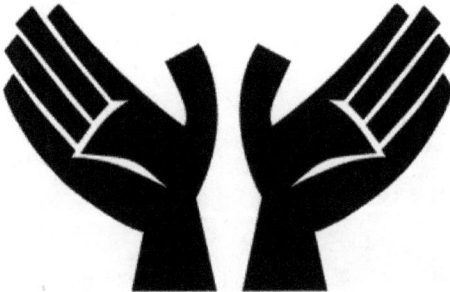

"Your Voice"

Your voice is over the waters;
It is the glory thunders,
And as Your voice thunders over the mighty waters.
Your voice is majestic,
It empowers others.
Your voice breaks the cedars.
It breaks in pieces the cedars all the way to Lebanon.
Your voice makes Lebanon leap like a calf;
And Sirion like a young wild ox.
Your voice strikes with flashes of lightning.
It shakes the desert all round.
Shaking the Desert of Kadesh.
Your voice twists the oaks,
And strips the forests bare.
Your voice is glorious,
No other voice can compare.

"Weeping and Rejoicing"

Weeping may stay for the entire night, but rejoicing
comes in the morning.

"Stop"

Stop beating yourself up.
Stop replaying the past.
Stop wondering or wishing on trivial things.
You have one life.
So, stop, think, and make it special.

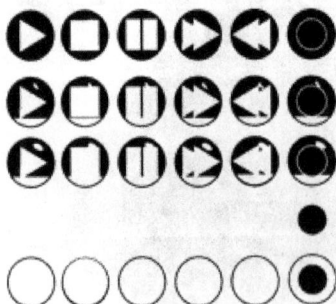

"Loving"

Loving others is better than being loved.

"Expectations"

The expectations we have for others, are premediated resentments. Therefore, it is better to give of ourselves with no expectation. For by doing so, we can be assured to receive good things beyond our wildest imaginations.

Day 327/365

"Thought for the Day"

The person who feels appreciated, will always do
more than expected.

Day 328/365

"A Good Marriage"

A good marriage is the one where each partner
secretly suspects that they got the better deal.
#humility #sacrificial love

"Procrastination"

Procrastination is the greatest labour-saving
invention of all time.

"Travel Therapy"

Don't you just wish that travel therapy was included
in our health insurance? Like, oh your tooth hurts?
Go to Switzerland. Oh, your eye hurts? Go to Paris.
Oh, your arm hurts? Go to America. Oh, your leg
hurts? Go to China. Oh, your back hurts? Go to
London. Oh, your heart hurts? Go to Egypt. Oh, your
brain hurts? Go to Australia. Oh, your whole life
hurts? Go to Heaven.

"Nerves"

There are a 100 billion nerves in our human body; and there are people who can aggravate all of them, at the same time.

"Video Game"

Life is like a videogame. No matter how good you get, or what level you go up to; you will always get zapped in the end.

"Receives, Finds and Opens"

For everyone who asks, receives.

For everyone who seeks, finds.

For everyone, who knocks, the door opens.

Day 334/365

"Success"

Small and consistent hard work daily, will transform to large success in one day.

"True Friends"

To have a true friend in this life, is a gift. It is the highest delight in this life.

To be a true friend in this life, is a noble honour. It is the most difficult undertakings in this life.

"Pain"

Stab me in my heart; once, twice, more.
You are hurting yourself in the end- much more.
Truth be told.
I am a strong person.
When I fall,
I rise stronger.
When I'm mistreated,
I do not feel sorry for myself.
Because I am a survivor.
Not a victim.
So even amid,
The past and present pain,
You'll see me laughing,
And smiling in the rain.

"The Broken"

The broken will always love harder than most. This is because the broken have been in the dark; so, they have learned to appreciate everything that shines.

"Tired"

Them: Are you okay?
You: Yes, I'm just 'tired'.

T-Terrified and Torn apart.
I-Insecure and Incomplete.
R-Restless and Really faking it.
E- Empty and Extremely sad.
D- Drowning in waves of Depression.

Them: So, you're good, then?

You: Yes.

"Treat Me like..."

Treat me like an average, and I'll make myself
a savage.
Treat me like a player, and I'll show you a coach.
Treat me like a fool, and I'll provide you with a tool.
Treat me like a hater, and I'll give you more to hate.
Treat me like a joke, and I'll leave you like it's funny.

"Fan Club"

People who talk behind people's back.
Notably behind my back.
Used to hurt me.
Like a lot.
But now.
With a shifted perspective.
I can say: Wow, I've got a fan club!

"Some people"

Some people create an aura of sunshine and joy wherever they go. And some people create an aura of sunshine and joy wherever they are absent. Strive to be the former kind of 'some people'.

"Marriage and Coffee"

My incredible marriage is like a cup of an almond latte (insert your favourite drink). I may have it every day, albeit sometimes twice a day. But I always look forward to it. And enjoy it.

"I Will Exalt You"

I will exalt You.
For you lifted me out of the depths,
And didn't let my enemies gloat over me.

I will exalt You.
I called to You for help,
And you speedily healed me.

I will exalt You.
You brought me up from the realm of the dead.
Sparing from going down to the pit- misery.

I will exalt You.
For Your anger lasts only a moment,
But Your grace, lasts a lifetime.

I will exalt You.
Weeping may stay for the night,
But rejoicing comes in the morning.

I will exalt You.
When I felt secure,
And when I feel shaken.

When You favoured me,
You made my royal mountain stand firm.
But when You hid your face from me,
I was dismayed.

I will exalt You.

For what is gained if I am silenced?
Will the dust praise you?
Will it proclaim your faithfulness?

Hear, and be merciful to me;
You turned my wailing into dancing;
You removed my sackcloth and clothed me with joy.

I will exalt You.
I cannot be silent.
I will exalt You, forever.

"As the..."

As the bee works for the good of others, so I work to
serve you.
As the sun shines every morning, so my smile lights
up the room.
As the bird looks for its home, so my heart looks
out for you.
As the moon gets light from behind it, so I owe my
light to you.
As the deer pants for the water, so my soul longs
after you.
As the flower blossoms in due time, so I yearn to
grow with you.

"Where are you now?"

I miss you.
Miss you so bad.
My soul thirsts for you,
Makes me so sad.
Where can I go?
Where are you now?

Tears have been my food,
Day and night.
While people say to me,
'You'll be alright'.
They mean well,
But I find no comfort.
Where are you now?
Why have you slumbered?

These things I remember
As I pour out my soul:
How I used to go to your house,
With no care at all.
Felt protected and at ease.
Friendship with you,
Was like therapy.
Where are you now?
For my soul, is down.
Yes, I have a storm in my mind.
Yet, I'm holding onto two questions,
Both that give me hope:
Where are you now?
And
When can I go?

"I Give it to You"

I give it to You:
My prayers and pleas.
I give it to You.
So hear and answer me.
My thoughts trouble me,
And I feel distraught
Everyone wants to be my enemy.
They say threats that steal my joy.

I give it to You.
When the wicked come;
They bring down suffering on me.
I give it to You.
When the people assail and
Don't take me seriously.

My heart is in anguish within me;
Feels like there is no end.
The terrors of death have fallen on me.
Creating fear and trembling again.

I give it to You.
You have beset me;
And are my witness alone.
I give it to You.
As horror has overwhelmed me.
Oh, how I wish I had the wings of a dove!
Then, I would fly away and be at rest.
Yes, I would fly far away,
Even in the tempest and storm,

Rather than be in this distress,
Surrounded but terribly alone.

I give it to You.
Confuse the wicked,
Confound their words against all.
For I see violence and strife;
Against big and small,.
In all cities and countries.
Day and night they prowl about on its walls;
Malice and abuse are within it.
What is more,
Destructive forces are at work,
Spitting threats and lies
That never leave its streets.

I give it to You.
When the enemy were insulting me.
With You, I can endure it;
Even when a foe rises,
I can hide.

I give it to You,
When a man like myself,
A companion, close friend,
Whom I once enjoyed sweet fellowship
At the house of God,
Stabs me in the back,
With no remorse in sight.

I give it to You.
You're my constant.
You always love and save me.
Making everything alright.

I give it to You.
Evening, morning, and noon
You rescue me unharmed
From the battle waged against me,
At all times.

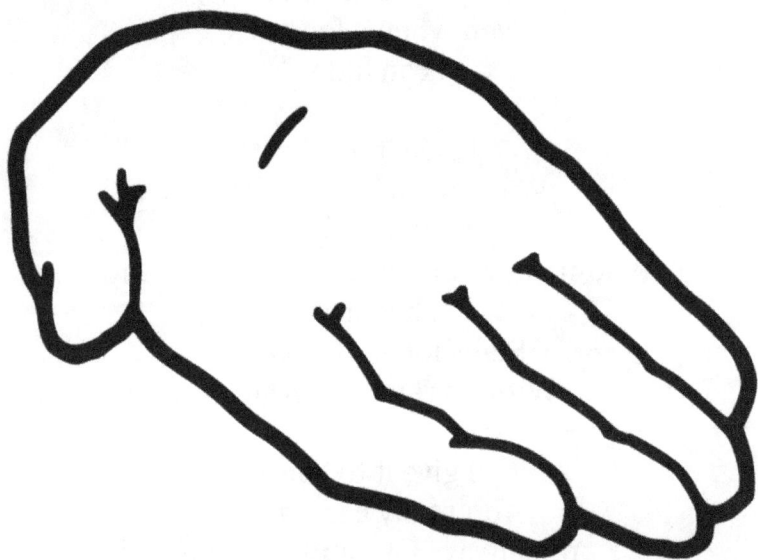

"Of What Are You Afraid?"

Of what are you afraid?
Maybe you're like me and scared of snakes, but
ironically not sharks. Or perhaps you're frightened by
the dark. Or the fact that not everyone in this life will
like you. Whatever the fear is, it is always best to ask
for help. For what good is it to cover up and pretend
you have your fears under control, when you can
humbly receive help?

"Judging"

Before judging another person, prove that you
are perfect.

"Attitude"

The more I grow and get experience, the more I appreciate the impact that attitude has in my life. No longer do I value the facts of any matter before delving into the attitude behind them. For attitude is more important than the facts. Attitude is more important than money, education, and circumstances. Attitude is more important than the number of failures and successes you can count or care to remember. Attitude has more power than knowledge; because I have witnessed how attitude can make or break many facets in our lives. Attitude can make or break a place of worship, a company, a workplace, a family, a marriage, and a friendship. We cannot change the past. We cannot change people. But what we can change, is our attitude. And in the words of Charles Swindoll, it is with you and I to change our attitudes; for the betterment of ourselves and everyone around us.

"MORE"

More sleep.
More hugs.
More kisses.
More humour.
More honesty.
More dreaming.
More love.
More kindness.
More fun.
More peace.
More trust.
More music.
More sunsets.
More joy.
More long walks.
More laughter.
More coffee.
More tea.
More road trips.
More things free.
More of You.
Less of Me.

"This is What it Feels Like"

So, this is what it feels like to fall out of love.
You're still there.
You exist in the world.
And I think about you from time to time.

So, this is what it feels like to wallow in pain.
I forget the things you did.
The way you hurt me.
And I still blame myself for how it ended.

So, this is what it feels like to not forgive.
I blame you for the pain I feel.
I avoid certain places that remind what we shared.
And I carry the hurt deep in my heart somewhere.

So, this is what it feels like to move on.
I take and revel all the memories.
I carry them as lessons in disguise.
And I know that I'm on my way to healing inside.

"Healed Wound"

Stop touching your wounds. Healing is born in the deep silence of untouched wounds.

Day 353/365

"Peace?"

All people will say that they 'want peace' on this world. But very few people work to make it so.

"Calmness is the Cradle of Power"

They say that calmness is the cradle of power.
And rightly so!
Calmness brings clarity to our mind.
Calmness creates strength to put aside the negative.
Calmness is the winner in consciousness.
Calmness brings balance,
And with balance, comes power.

"Pythagoras Theory Shifted"

As long as men massacre animals, they will kill each other. Indeed, he who sows the seeds of murder and pain, cannot reap the joy of love.

SOW

REAP

"Life Changes as You do Too"

Life changes as you do too.
You stay friends forever.
You lose friends sometimes.
You realize some people were never really your
friend at times.

Life changes as you do too.
You find love that lasts forever.
You look for another love.
You lose love.
You realize that all along you were searching
When you were already loved- a lot.

Life changes as you do too.
You laugh out loud no matter how odd it sounds.
You cry like it's your last day sticking around.

Life changes as you do too.
You do this.
You do that.
You do things you are proud of;
As much as things you wish you had.

Life changes as you do too.
Sometimes you love life,
Wishing it was long as can be.
Then other times, you hate life,
Wishing it'd be more easy.

Life changes as you do too.

So, take a minute to remember your worth:
You are priceless all the time.
And no matter what life throws at you,
You are made to thrive.

Day 357/365

"Self- Acceptance"

No one needs anyone's affection or approval. When
someone rejects or abandons us, it's about them. It's
about them and their insecurities. It's about them
and their shortcomings. It's about them and their
needs unmet. You're allowed to voice your thoughts
and feelings. You exist; therefore, you matter. You're
allowed to hold onto the truth that who you are is
exactly enough. And with that, you're allowed to
remove anyone from your life who makes you feel
otherwise.

"Time"

Time stays long enough for anyone who will use it.

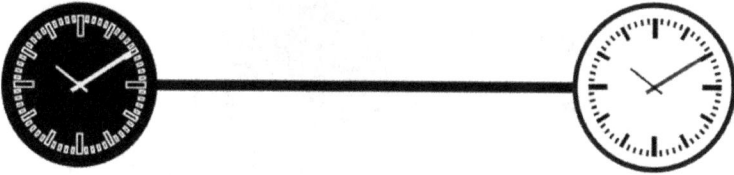

"This is What You Don't Do"

Don't let the world make you bitter.
Don't let the actions of others, make you cold inside.
Things will happen to hurt us.
People will come and leave us.
Don't let the negatives make you unkind.
It's okay to cry.
It's okay to be upset.
We're human.
We break.
We make mistakes.
But don't let pain and sadness ruin your life.
There are moments in your life where you feel like
giving up.
But don't give up.
Exhale.
I know you're weak.

But the things that show your weak side,
Are the things that'll make you stronger.
This life is all about learning by going.
So, keep going

Day 360/365

"Saint Augustine's Travelling Approval"

The world is a book and those who do not travel,
read only one page.

"Forever"

No matter how painful the distance can be, not having you in my life forever would be worse. And yes, forever is a long time; but I would be honoured to spend forever with you by my side.

"Life Advice"

Always be the best person you can be.
Be kind even when you're tired.
Be understanding even when you're angry.
Do more than you're asked.
Go the extra mile.
Go out of your way to do things for people.
Don't silently expect anything in return either.
Just give abundantly.
Be a good human generously.
The good people in this life are like moths;
They are attracted to the flame of spirit and light.
Be the light.
Keep your spirit.
Live your life today and every day,
As if it was your last day.

Day 363/365

"Beauty"

A thing of beauty is never perfect.

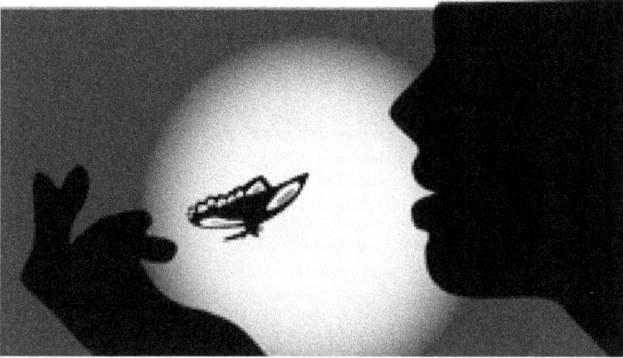

Day 364/365

"Planting a Seed"

You cannot force someone to comprehend a message that they are not ready to receive. At the same time, you must not underestimate the power of planting the seed.

"Kingdom of Heaven"

The Kingdom of Heaven isn't a destination. The Kingdom of Heaven lives in you; and will reveal itself when you truly know yourself and accept it.